The
INSIDER'S
DOSSIER

HOW TO USE *LEGAL* INSIDER TRADING TO MAKE BIG STOCK PROFITS

The
[INSIDER'S DOSSIER]

HOW TO USE *LEGAL* INSIDER TRADING TO MAKE BIG STOCK PROFITS

By Andrew Packer

Humanix Books

www.humanixbooks.com
Boca Raton, FL, USA

Humanix Books
P.O. Box 20989
West Palm Beach, FL 33416
USA
www.humanixbooks.com
email: info@humanixbooks.com

Humanix Books is a division of Humanix Publishing LLC. Its trademark, consisting of the words "Humanix Books" is registered in the U.S. Patent and Trademark Office and in other countries.

Printed in the United States of America and the United Kingdom.

ISBN (Paperback) 978-1-63006-020-6
ISBN (E-book) 978-1-63006-021-3

Library of Congress Control Number 2014930395

Contents

Section II:
Beyond Insider Trading – Other Factors to Look For

Foreword

When you're a business news journalist as I used to be, you get to meet and interview a lot of CEOs and other high-profile magnates. I've been lucky enough to ask questions of Bill Gates, Warren Buffett, Michael Dell, Intel's Andy Grove, Southwest Airlines founder Herb Kelleher, Ted Turner, Richard Branson, and countless others.

Some you chat with in person; others you talk with on the phone, on a satellite video connection, or at a press conference. The one thing all of these highly successful individuals have in common: Each has an idea to sell.

Sometimes they're selling a theme: "My company is growing fast — we have many quarters of rapid expansion still ahead."

Other times they're trying to revive the firm's reputation: "The restructure is going perfectly according to plan, even though we just lost millions more in red ink last quarter."

And still others aim to downplay expectations and manufacture a surprise turnaround with an upcoming profit report: "Things are beginning to look better, but keep in mind that we're expecting lots of positive change between now and next quarter . . ."

What does all of this have to do with a book about tracking the share-buying activities of corporate "insiders" (the CEOs and others who make up a company's leadership)? Plenty, because here's something else you realize after following the comings and goings of top executives: Almost anyone who's a good talker, with a well-cut Brooks Brothers suit (not to mention a top-notch stylist and a good manicure), can act the part of the CEO. That's easy.

But when it comes to actually creating shareholder wealth . . . Well, that's something else entirely. Sure, the CEO can follow the standard corporate strategy playbook: Is an underperforming division holding back growth? Sell it off. Moribund stock price? Restructure the company. Long-term growth rates are slowing? Refocus on new profit opportunities.

That's all well and good, but are those viable strategies? For every successful turnaround, a dozen others never pan out. Why? Because of poor decisions by upper management. And that's something that can't be fixed — no matter how many press releases are issued, or how often the CEO appears on the financial news programs.

That's why it's so important not to follow what executives *say*, but rather what they *do* with their money.

I'm not talking about stock options (which many companies dole out like candy, costing them nothing), but cold hard cash. That's money already earned by the board members and executive team that they're now reinvesting back into their company's equity base.

When you start seeing that happen, that's when the probabilities for creating sustainable shareholder wealth begin looking a lot better. In betting parlance, the corporate types and the shareholders all have their money riding on the same horse.

So that's the goal: finding companies where the corporate insiders are personally buying their stock in significant quantities. But, like many things on Wall Street, even that simple equation is a lot more complex than it appears.

That's why you'll be happy to have Andrew Packer, editor of Newsmax Media's Insider Hotline Newsletter, to guide you through the ins and outs of this investing strategy.

Keep in mind that there are literally thousands of publicly-held companies. And they file scores of documents with federal regulators disclosing their executives' inside trades. Andrew shows you how to find the valuable nuggets buried within that mountain of insider trading data. He cuts through all the extraneous "noise" and demonstrates how to profit alongside all those bullish corporate executives — i.e., when to buy, and how much.

Just who is Andrew Packer? He's one of those rare people who has a sort of natural instinct for investing and a keen eye for wealth-building. That's why Andrew learned the importance of growing wealth and putting time on his side by investing at a young age, starting with precious-metals investing before the age of 10 and building a stock portfolio before the age of 13. Today, Andrew invests in everything from stocks, real estate, and mutual funds/ETFs (exchange-traded funds), to commodities and options.

Along the way, Andrew acquired a BA in economics and has honed his analytical skills, working in real estate research and private equity. Even while working, he's found the time to experiment with different investment strategies (one of his most powerful strategies is revealed in Chapter 9 of this book). Andrew is currently editor of the Financial Braintrust with Moneynews, a frequent contributor to the Financial Intelligence Report Newsletter (which he also used to edit), and editor of the Options Trader investment service.

Andrew is author of the runaway bestseller *Aftershock's High Income Guide*, which has helped hundreds of thousands of readers start generating meaningful income at today's low interest rates. In 2012, he wrote *Uncharted: Your Guide to Investing in the Age of Uncertainty*, which looked at the challenges — and opportunities — investors face in the current, precarious global economy.

As an investor, Andrew approaches the market with a high level of concern for risk, following the tried and true investment advice from the "Oracle of Omaha" himself, Warren Buffet:

Rule #1: Never lose money.

Rule #2: Never forget rule number 1.

That's partly why Andrew is such a big fan of investing alongside bullish insiders. It puts the odds in your favor. But it's not just the win/loss ratio of insider trades — it's the market-crushing returns you can obtain as well.

After reading Andrew's guide, you're sure to come away with a unique understanding of this highly lucrative investment strategy.

And better yet, you'll be a smarter, wiser, more profitable investor who knows how to boost his or her investment returns while lowering risk at the same time.

Jeff Yastine
Director of Financial Newsletters, *Moneynews*

Introduction: Decoding the Mystery of the Public Room

"An investment in knowledge pays the best interest."
— *Benjamin Franklin*

In the middle of Washington, DC, a moderately tall building holds one of the best known sources of financial information. With this information, anyone with a brokerage account has the tools he or she needs to handily beat the market year after year.

Yes, it's a government building, but it's not the US Treasury — they don't even handle money in there. That's the responsibility the Bureau of Engraving and Printing, which could hardly be confused with the building to which I'm referring. Nor is this could this building be confused with the Federal Reserve building. The Fed is slowly becoming more public about its monetary policy, but it's still not as transparent as this particular agency.

This building is at 100 F Street, NE, right by Union Station, just north of the Capitol Building. Flagpoles stand formidably outside the entrance, as do security guards.

It even has a room set aside for the public. Naturally, the government named it the Public Room.

While most of the building is off-limits to anyone not strictly working for the government or on government business, you can find (or if necessary, request) within this room whatever information you need. Why? Because this agency exists to acquire and disseminate this information to anyone with an interest in learning it.

The information available from this government agency is vast. In an average year, its data reporting is increased by over 270,000 forms. In a country with a population of more than 315 million, that may not seem like a lot. But it is staggering when you consider that only 15,000 organizations are required to file information here.

Yes, some of the information this agency receives is held back from the public. But what's astonishing is how much of the data collected is available to anyone who walks in . . . *free of charge.*

The government agency is the US Securities and Exchange Commission (SEC), and the data collected and disseminated is based on insider trades. This includes purchases, sales, and simple disclosures of ownership.

Chances are you've heard that investing alongside insiders can help boost your returns. In this guide, we'll look at insider trades. Specifically, we'll find out how buying shares alongside high-level executives, board of director members, and major shareholders (those with a 10 percent or larger stake) can give you higher returns than the market.

Most investors and fund managers can't even beat the market year over year. They chase stocks that have performed well right before those stocks crash. Yet corporate insiders have a consistent track record of trouncing the market. That's why this information is so powerful — provided you know how to decode it.

Before we delve into the details, here are the key takeaways on insider trading:

These insider trades are legal. (We'll look at the specific differences between a legal and an illegal insider trading in Chapter 3.) The entire point of creating the SEC was to ensure that the public received materially important information on a company as soon as its officers, directors, and major shareholders did. Hence the strict reporting requirements for every trade — even a trade as small as buying or selling one share!

These insider trades beat the market average consistently. On average, a portfolio of stocks based on insider buying will beat the market by 6 percentage points per year. Of course, if you know how to read the data, you could avoid some of the insider buys that go awry — and do even better than those "in the know" execs! Imagine making 20 percent from a stock in only three months; or making 42 percent gains buying a stock before it realizes record-smashing earnings; or even using some of the more advanced strategies in this guide, making triple-digit gains while putting far less capital at risk.

These insider trades are easy to follow . . . and getting easier every year. For decades, professional investors have had an information advantage. They've been able to get this data faster than mom-and-pop investors. This information edge has enabled them to achieve even better returns by getting into trades alongside insiders more quickly. But that's changing. Today, regular investors can get the information faster and cheaper than ever before. This narrowing advantage between professionals and insiders isn't completely gone yet, but it's getting there.

But there's a catch. And it's a big one. This information is public . . . but it's encoded. To understand this information and how to profit from it, the data must first be interpreted. What's more, once you have decoded it, you need to know how to apply it to your brokerage account to get the full financial benefit that it offers.

Between the layers of government forms and Wall Street lingo, that can be a tough prospect. But it's not impossible. In this guide, we'll decode the secrets of the public room, find a way to access the information without taking regular trips to Washington, DC, and even look beyond this information to better improve investment returns.

I've divided this book into two sections. In the first, we'll look at the hard data behind insider trading: how (and why) it outperforms the market indexes, and how you can narrow that data down to the profitable essentials. In part two, I'll show you how make the strategy of following corporate insider buys even more profitable by examining some other very important factors.

I

The Insider Edge

1

The Benefits of
Insider Trading

"You want more insider trading, not less. You want to give the people most likely to have knowledge about deficiencies of the company an incentive to make the public aware of that."

— *Milton Friedman*

In the 1987 movie *Wall Street*, the arch-capitalist Gordon Gekko addresses an annual meeting for Teldar Paper, the firm he's been buying shares of hand over fist to become the largest single holder of stocks.

In a room full of everyone from guys in suits to little old ladies who own a few shares, he spells out part of the problem with the company: the proliferation of management. In his address to the shareholders, Gekko reveals that the company has nearly three dozen vice presidents and that all they seem to do is send reports back and forth to each other. Their salaries? Over $200,000 per year.

Gekko points out that part of the reason why the company is faltering is because that money could be put to better use for the shareholders. By the end of Gekko's speech, which includes the best-known line in the film, the audience is applauding.

Insider Advantage No. 1: Aligned Interests Between Management and Shareholders

Fast-forward 25 years and nothing's really changed. One of the biggest problems with corporate America is with its management. Simply put, there tends to be a conflict of interest between the managers of a company, such as the CEO, CFO, and Board of Directors, versus that of the shareholders, who actually own the company.

Shareholders want the company to grow, to continue paying a dividend (if it's paying one), and so on. But most major companies have thousands of shareholders, so their voice is diffused. Management wants to get paid, and handsomely so, for the work it does. Shareholders don't have a say in day-to-day management, whereas the executives do.

Sometimes, however, management's interest is aligned with that of the shareholders. Typically, this happens when a manager or managers own a large percentage of the company. The standard-bearer is Warren Buffett, who has maintained control of Berkshire Hathaway for nearly half a century.

But most owner-operators who own such a substantial stake in a business are rare. It's more common for corporate executives to receive stock options as a form of compensation, which they can cash out and pay capital gains taxes on, rather than taking the hit of higher income tax rates.

That's why the bulk of insider transactions, as reported to the SEC, are sales. Fair enough. Insiders have plenty of reasons to sell. It's part of their remuneration.

Furthermore, investors' wealth should never be tied up in only one company, especially one they work at. Enron employees who contributed to their 401(k) plan ended up getting burned twice when the company went under — they lost their jobs and their Enron stock went to zero. Diversification is important, even for employees of the most financially secure companies.

Finally, corporate insiders may cash out simply to buy a new home, take a vacation, buy a sports car, put a kid through college, pay for a divorce, and so on.

So what reasons do corporate insiders have to buy shares of their company on the open market? Really just one: the expectation of higher share prices in the future.

It's a powerful incentive aligned with their specialized knowledge. High-level corporate insiders know when sales are going well before it becomes a materially important statement. They may have a gut feel for how a hot new product is going to perform. They know before the market if a major customer just left a competitor for them.

They might know that a recent downgrade from a Wall Street firm was based on outdated information and the wrong conclusion.

The specifics might matter to some financial analysts, but insiders don't have to disclose the specific reason why they're buying — it still comes down to the fact that they expect the share price to go higher.

Insider Advantage No. 2: Market-Beating Returns

Let's get down to business. When it comes to investing, higher percentage returns are better than lower returns. Of course, there's a trade-off: Investments that beat the average market returns in a given year tend to have a higher risk to them.

Much of this risk can be mitigated over time. You'll never lose money in stocks over a 20-year period or longer. But anything shorter means having a risk-management plan in place. If you need cash in a few months, it's too risky to invest in stocks when you could be invested in cash, short-term notes, or certificates of deposit instead.

Investing with corporate insiders confers a huge advantage to investment returns over the short term, while at the same time lowering risk.

When you invest alongside corporate insiders, you can easily obtain market-beating investment returns within a matter of days, or weeks in some cases. For the most part, the advantages of insider trading play out over periods of a few months to a year.

As for the risk — yes, some insider trades won't perform well. But a study analyzing aggregate insider purchase activity for the 20 years between 1974 and 1994 revealed that simply investing an equal amount of money into every insider purchase would lead to a market-beating return 75 percent of the time.

In only five of those 20 years did buying alongside insiders lead to a worse performance than the market, but the worst underperformance was by only 2.1 percent, and two of the five underperforming years lagged by less than 1 percent.

So by investing alongside insiders, you're betting on a strategy that beats the market 75 percent of the time. That's a great way to boost returns. You can further reduce the risk of underperforming the market average by weeding through trades to cherry-pick only the ones that send the strongest buy signals. We'll look more closely at strategies to do just that in Section 2 of this book.

When it comes to insider trading, that's what you get. Market-beating returns that, even in down years for the market, let you keep your shirt.

That's all great in theory and based on historical data, but with most studies on the benefits of insider trading being made before the most recent financial crisis, it's important to ask: Does this strategy still work today?

The answer is a resounding yes. It might work even better today, as there are ways to filter out a lot of the static of insider trading to get to the absolute best opportunities.

Now let's step away from theory and statistics to reveal the practical application of the insider advantage.

The Insider Advantage in Practice

EXAMPLE NO. 1: A 54 PERCENT GAIN WITHIN A WEEK!

On July 30, 2013, Will Weinstein of Hansen Medical (HNSN) bought over $1 million in his company's stock, picking up 869,825 shares at an average price of $1.23 per share. That's a pretty big bet on a company with a $120 million market cap — Weinstein's buy was for nearly 1 percent of the entire company!

He wasn't alone. Other corporate officers picked up shares as

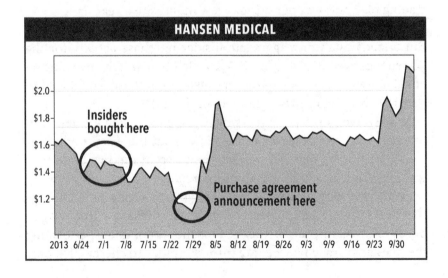

well at open market prices. What did these insiders know? That the company's financial future was in good hands. In late July, the company reported that it entered into a purchase agreement with Oracle Investment Management for the tidy sum of $93 million. That sent shares surging by 54 percent within a week.

Take a closer look at the chart of Hansen's move. Investors reading through the SEC's Form 4s, which record changes in an insider's holdings, had plenty of time to get in. In fact, this is one of the rare instances where individual investors could have gotten even better returns than the insiders themselves!

EXAMPLE NO. 2: STRONG INSIDER BUYING FOR A COMPANY ON THE MEND

Multiple insiders have been bullish on Equal Energy (EQU) throughout 2013. The Canadian company, which owns oil- and natural-gas producing assets in Oklahoma, finally turned a corner toward profitability after years of losses. A cut dividend was reinstated, with a relatively high yield to boot.

But even as the share price started to rise, insiders continued to buy shares. Indeed, there's been insider buying by corporate officers throughout the year — each and every month. Some of those buys have been option exercises, but many have been open market buys.

Although shares rose over 55 percent through 2013, as long as insiders remain bullish, there's still the strong likelihood that the market-beating gains will continue at this small-cap energy firm.

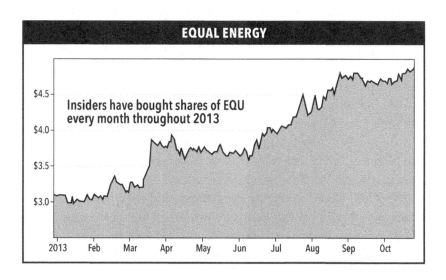

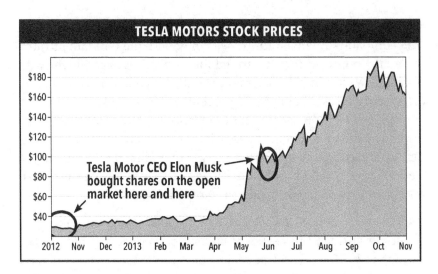

TESLA MOTORS STOCK PRICES

Tesla Motor CEO Elon Musk bought shares on the open market here and here

INSIDER ADVANTAGE NO. 3: 453 PERCENT GAINS ON THIS MISUNDERSTOOD COMPANY

On May 30, 2013, Tesla Motors (TSLA) CEO Elon Musk bought 1,084,129 shares at an average price of $92.24 per share. Four months later, by the end of September 2013, shares were up a staggering 84.25 percent. Not bad for a 125-day return!

But that wasn't Musk's first buy-in on the open market. On October 3, 2012, the CEO made a million-dollar bet by buying 35,398 shares at $28.25 per share. The returns on those shares, through the end of September 2013, rose a staggering 453.48 percent!

While shares of the automaker are down a bit from their September highs, it's important to note that this level of market-beating returns is rare. It's the kind of surprise move in a stock that shocks just about everyone except those who have their finger on the company's pulse on a daily basis — i.e., its executive officers.

What's more, anyone looking at Tesla based on its fundamentals (myself included) would have reached the conclusion that the stock was overpriced both times the CEO bought in. Anyone looking at the technical charts of the stock at the time Musk bought would have stayed on the sidelines too.

All of the above examples are recent, and they confirm earlier academic studies on the relative outperformance of insider trading. Indeed, as a variety of academic and financial journals have reported, bullish insiders tend to beat the average return of the stock market by anywhere from 6 to 10 percent per year.

Of course, the actual percentage may vary, depending on the sector, the overall return of the stock market, and so forth. For instance, a study from UCLA and NYU nearly a decade ago revealed that a group of insider buyers in the technology and pharmaceutical sectors beat the average stock market indexes by 9.6 percent in the six months following their purchases.

I've found that weighing in the few trades that underperform across every investment sector, investors today should expect about an 8 percent relative outperformance versus the overall stock market.

In 2013, with the S&P 500 index up more than 23 percent, the average insider-based buy returned over 30 percent. In some of the market's down years, the relative outperformance of insider buys meant smaller losses.

Worst-case scenario, it's closer to the low range of 6 percent per year. But that's still a huge level of outperformance! Over time, this advantage is clear. An investor with a $50,000 nest egg in index funds earning the market average of 8 percent per year will end up with $246,340 in 20 years.

That's not bad.

But with the worst-case scenario of outperforming the market by only 6 percent per year above the market average makes for a 14 percent annual return. That same $50,000 compounded over

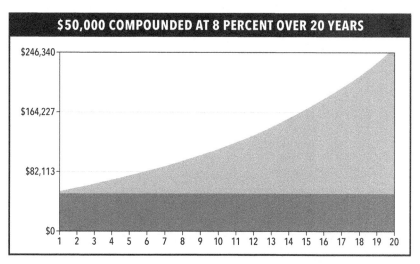

$50,000 COMPOUNDED AT 8 PERCENT OVER 20 YEARS

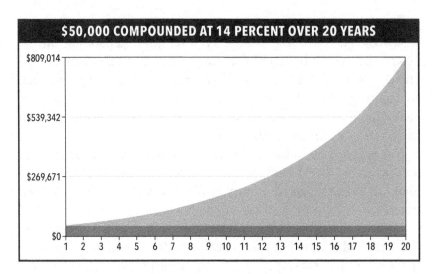

$50,000 COMPOUNDED AT 14 PERCENT OVER 20 YEARS

20 years will grow to be **more than three times larger!** The total comes out to just over $800,000!

That's the real power of investing alongside insiders. It's not just any single trade; it's the power of using this tool repeatedly to beat the market year after year.

This strategy is safe. And over time, it's powerful.

In the next chapter, we'll look at the illegal side of insider trading. It accounts for less than a fraction of 1 percent of insider trades, yet it's the one that gets the headlines and scares investors away from this powerful strategy.

2

The Difference Between Legal and Illegal Insider Trading

"It takes a crook to catch a crook."
— *FDR about Joseph P. Kennedy (father of JFK) on why he was appointed inaugural chairman of the SEC.*

Now that you've seen the benefits of insider trading and what it can do for your portfolio, remember that all of the prior examples are not only safe ways to increase your wealth, but they're legal ways as well.

The SEC has gone out of its way to ensure that insiders have the opportunity to voice their opinion on their firm's prospects with their wallet. At the same time, the SEC comes down hard on insiders who use their knowledge to profit before the public can.

That's because the SEC has two critical criteria for illegal insider trading. An illegal insider trade is one that is done with materially important information. This could be something like whether or not a company will make its estimated earnings for the next quarter, or whether a massive dividend or share buyback is going to be implemented.

The next criterion is that this information is used before it has been disclosed to the public. Given the information that high-ranking corporate executives come across every day, even a series of non-materially important information may cause someone to think again about buying or selling shares in their company.

To some extent, these two requirements can appear vague. And legal cases on insider trading have had a tough time drawing the exact line. However, it's an improvement on a system where the abuses occurred without the requirement of prompt and full disclosures.

Prior to the creation of the SEC in the 1930s, corporate insiders could buy or sell shares without having to disclose that information to the public. An opportunistic corporate officer might talk up the company's bright future while quickly selling shares before investors learned the bleak reality.

Such practices, if discovered, could lead to charges of fraud. A 1909 Supreme Court decision ruled that a corporate director who bought company shares before they jumped in price had committed fraud by not disclosing his inside information.

Besides insider trading that involves material and non-public information, corporate insiders are forbidden from making two other types of transactions.

The first is short sales. Simply put, corporate insiders can't sell shares of their company short. If they think their company stock is going to go down, they can sell off all their shares. Unlike day traders, if they think there's more downside, they can't sell shares they don't own at market with the hope of closing out their short position later.

Next, there's a thing called short-swing transactions. That's when an insider buys or sells shares within a six-month period. The intention would obviously be to make quick profits on short-term corporate events. It's important to note that this type of transaction only affects the direct purchase or sale of stocks on the open market. It doesn't include the receiving and cashing out of stock options.

So how are these illegal insider trades caught? Let's look at a few examples and see, beginning with the most famous insider trading case of all time . . .

Not Even an Insider: The Martha Stewart Case

In July 2004, home decorating guru Martha Stewart was sentenced to five months in prison for insider trading. In December 2001 she had sold $229,513 worth of ImClone shares — her entire stake — on the recommendation of her broker, Peter Bacanovic.

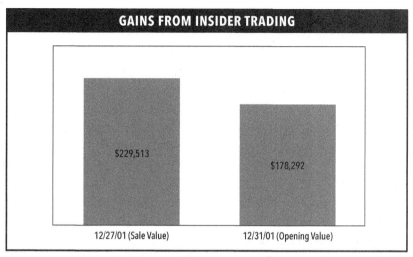

Based on ImClone's change in stock price, by selling early, Martha Stewart managed to avoid _$51,221 in potential losses_.

Bacanovic had obtained information that one of ImClone's drugs failed to get FDA approval, and that it would be announced shortly. The founder and CEO of ImClone, Samuel Waksal, was preparing to dump the shares he and his other family members owned.

Four days after Stewart sold her shares, ImClone shares tumbled, saving Stewart $51,221 in potential losses. Based on her total net worth, this saved about 0.1 percent of her wealth.

Stewart claimed that she had a standing order to sell shares of ImClone if they fell below $60 at any point, and she used that as a basis for her defense at trial. Stewart hit up the media circuit for support, starting a website and taking out a full-page advertisement in *USA Today* (which cost more than the $51,000 she saved with her trade) to send out an open letter of her innocence.

In her ad she stated: "I want you to know that I am innocent — and that I will fight to clear my name . . . The government's attempt to criminalize these actions makes no sense to me . . . I am confident I will be exonerated of these baseless charges."

Stewart wasn't the only one making a defense. Many questioned whether someone without direct insider knowledge should be prosecuted. Indeed, the US government's cost to prosecute (and eventually incarcerate) Stewart ran into the hundreds of thousands of dollars.

Although Stewart could have been sentenced to years in prison, she was sentenced to five months, followed by five months' home detention, two years' probation, and a $30,000 fine. Her bigger losses were in her executive-level position at her company as a result of being convicted of insider trading, and having to resign her position as a member of the board of directors of the New York Stock Exchange.

Indeed, when considering Martha Stewart's overall stock portfolio in December 2001, just as the tech bubble was bursting, it's plain to see that her investment portfolio was mostly in the red, with ImClone as her largest gain.

By selling a position with a gain, particularly in the last quarter of the year, Stewart would also be able to close out some losses and offset the capital gains taxes.

Indeed, as Stewart told a friend after selling the ImClone shares: "Just took lots of huge losses to offset some gains, made my stomach turn."

Nevertheless, the prosecution's case rested on the fact Stewart should have known there was illegal insider information being passed around by Bacanovic that insiders were dumping their shares.

Bacanovic received the same five-month prison sentence and five-month home detention sentence as Stewart, as well as a $4,000 fine.

Samuel Waksal was sentenced to seven years and three months in prison and ordered to pay more than $4 million in fines for his role. He was released in 2009.

The lesson here is that if you trade based on illegal insider information, the government will prosecute you even if it costs far more than the illegal gain.

The Largest Insider Trading Ring in History

On October 16, 2009, Raj Rajaratnam was arrested for insider trading and conspiring with a network to commit insider trading in the stock of multiple publicly traded companies. The total profits (and avoided losses) were put at approximately $60 million, making it the largest case of hedge fund, insider trading in history.

Rajaratnam, the Sri Lankan-born founder of the hedge fund Galleon Group, rose quickly through the ranks at organizations such as Chase Manhattan Bank and Needham & Company. His net worth

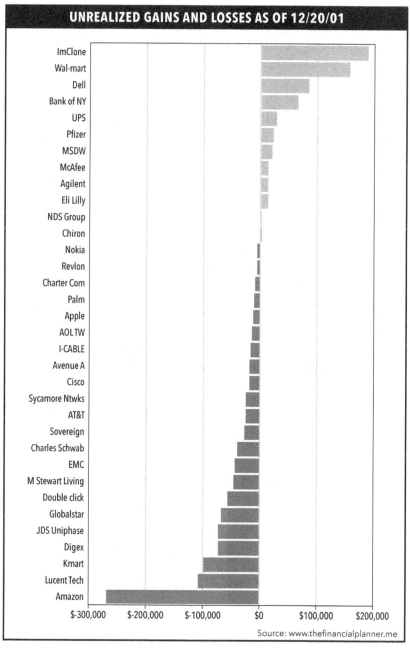

UNREALIZED GAINS AND LOSSES AS OF 12/20/01

Source: www.thefinancialplanner.me

Martha Stewart's stock portfolio was tanking. She sold shares of her most profitable investment. With most of her wealth tied up outside the stock market, the profits she locked in represented only 0.1 percent of her wealth. Is this the portfolio of someone benefiting from illegal insider trading?

climbed rapidly after starting Galleon Group, peaking at $1.8 billion in 2009, making him the 236th richest American according to Forbes. His fund managed a net annualized return of 22.3 percent according to a 2009 investor letter.

But apparently that wasn't enough.

According to the SEC, Rajaratnam received insider information from Robert Moffat of IBM, at one time considered for the position of CEO; Anil Kumar, senior executive at McKinsey & Company; Rajiv Goel at Intel Capital; and Roomy Khan of Intel. The SEC also alleged that Rajaratnam was trying to obtain information on the $5 billion in Goldman Sachs preferred shares bought by Warren Buffett (via Berkshire Hathaway).

At trial, Rajaratnam declined to take the stand. However, damning evidence from texts, voice mails, recordings, and witnesses ensured a conviction. At one point during the trial, a tape was played on which Rajaratnam stated, "I heard yesterday from somebody who's on the board of Goldman Sachs that they are going to lose $2 per share."

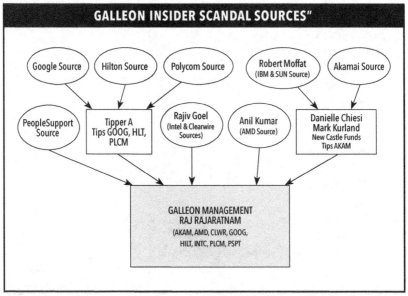

Source: U.S. Securities and Exchange Commission

Raj Rajaratnam was the recipient of illegal insider information from a variety of sources across multiple companies. The network was so wide, that investigators were still following up leads two years after Rajaratnam's conviction.

Raj Rajaratnam was sentenced to 11 years in prison in October 2011 after 12 days of jury deliberation. His conviction was upheld on appeal. Rajaratnam was also ordered to pay a fine of $10 million and forfeit $53.8 million.

The members of Rajaratnam's network also received relatively long prison sentences. Other cases of insider trading have emerged as a result of cracking this network, and these are still being investigated or tried as this book is being written, including investigations into SAC capital, which had to pay a $1.1 billion fine in 2013 for insider-related acts.

How to Get Caught: Absurdly Incriminating Statements

In April 2011, Garrett Bauer, a trader, and Matthew Kluger, a mergers and acquisitions attorney, were arrested and charged with insider trading. At the time of their arrests, the FBI believed that Kluger disclosed information to Bauer about the mergers his law firm was working on. One example included a tip that Sun Microsystems would buy Oracle.

It's believed that Kluger began sharing insider information when he was still a law student at NYU back in 1995, disclosing information on the upcoming merger between Lotus Development Corporation and IBM.

Over the next seventeen years, the information would come in sporadically (between 1999 and 2005 Kluger had no access to merger information). But often, Bauer simply wouldn't trade. In an interview with Walter Pavlo of Forbes, Bauer states:

"At first, it was about the money. When I started trading, I was broke and used credit card advances to make some trades. So Ken's [Robinson] tips were helpful at first, but the amounts [gains] were still small.

Over time, I had come up with my own day-trading strategies that made money by moving in and out of stocks throughout the day. That's why I didn't like Ken's tips because they were not that accurate. I would have to hold stocks for longer periods of time with him . . . sometimes it was months, when I was usually in a stock position for only a few minutes."

In other words, for a fast-paced trader like Bauer, insider trading was slow and stodgy. Indeed, getting into a trade before a merger was announced often meant sitting on a loss.

Both Kluger and Bauer were approached by the SEC over the course of their insider trading relationship, but they didn't make a move.

The total take on this trading was estimated at $32 million over the course of several years. In order to conceal their partnership in crime for so long, they used a middleman, Kenneth Robinson (who was a mortgage broker), pre-paid cell phones, and pay phones.

What Bauer and Kluger didn't know was that Robinson recorded their emails, phone calls, and other contacts after he agreed to cooperate with the FBI and SEC. In short, another form of insider information was leaking out.

Once Bauer traded on the information, he'd take the profits out in cash via ATMs. In one instance, Bauer stated that, if questioned about the hundreds of thousands in cash he was withdrawing, he would claim, "I used that as spending money. I don't know, I will say I bought prostitutes if it came down to that."

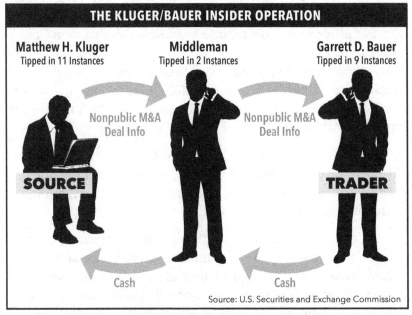

THE KLUGER/BAUER INSIDER OPERATION

Matthew H. Kluger
Tipped in 11 Instances

Middleman
Tipped in 2 Instances

Garrett D. Bauer
Tipped in 9 Instances

Nonpublic M&A Deal Info

Nonpublic M&A Deal Info

SOURCE

TRADER

Cash

Cash

Source: U.S. Securities and Exchange Commission

By using an intermediary, M&A attorney Matthew Kluger was able to pass on information to trader Garrett Bauer. Although this went on for a long time, the SEC eventually discovered the middleman and used him to obtain a record-breaking conviction.

Or, there's this gem between Bauer and Robinson regarding how they could literally launder the money:

Bauer: "We have to get all the fingerprints off that money."

Robinson: "Yeah."

Bauer: "Like you wearing gloves or something and wiping every bill down or something. But it has to be done. Or as, like, you giving it to me and me wiping every bill down."

Robinson: "You know something. Somebody did say, 'Why don't you just run it through a dish-, a dish-washing machine?'"

Bauer: "Well, I don't know. I mean, I've seen that in the movies but I don't know — who said that? Someone said that to you?"

Robinson: "Yeah, my cousin did. He goes, 'Run it through a washing machine.' And I'm like, "You can do that?' And he goes, 'Yeah.' And I go, 'Alright.'"

In 2012, Bauer pleaded guilty and was sentenced to nine years in federal prison. Kluger was sentenced to 12 years, a record for insider trading cases. Robinson, the informant to the FBI and SEC, got a relatively light 27-month sentence.

Folks, if these smart, Ivy League-educated lawyers and Wall Street traders could say and do such stupid things to make a few bucks, you really don't have to worry about the scourge of insider trading. With financial monitoring in place, most of the people inclined to do a few unethical things don't do it to begin with. The lesson here is clear. Those who are greedy enough to go ahead with illegal insider trading eventually get caught.

Conclusion: Illegal Insider Trading Will Catch up With Wrongdoers

Remember, these above examples make up most of the news headlines on insider trading, but they're by far the exception rather than the rule.

For instance, look at the chart on page 10. It shows SEC data on the number of enforcement actions it takes annually. As you can see, it averages less than 60 per year.

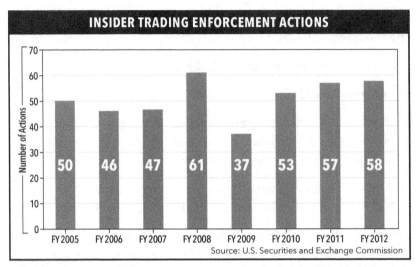

INSIDER TRADING ENFORCEMENT ACTIONS

FY 2005	FY 2006	FY 2007	FY 2008	FY 2009	FY 2010	FY 2011	FY 2012
50	46	47	61	37	53	57	58

Source: U.S. Securities and Exchange Commission

The SEC enforces around 50 cases on average annually, meaning that illegal insider trades account for less than 1/100th of 1 percent of insider transactions.

The conclusion is pretty clear. **Of the approximately 270,000 insider transactions reported to the SEC annually, illegal insider trading constitutes less than one one-hundredth of one percent.** Yes, a few of these cases make big headlines, but they're by far the minority. It's akin to how the nightly news might report a gruesome murder in a given day, but it doesn't mention the obvious fact that more than 300 million Americans had, well, an average day.

Yes, these headline-grabbing stories are far more interesting than the ones about consistently beating the market over time with a more humdrum approach of following legal insider trades. And folks like nothing more than a story about some wealthy person's fall from grace. But it's a distraction from the overwhelming majority of legal insider trades that can quietly make you a fortune without landing you in hot water.

Moreover, the kind of insider trading that gets CEOs hauled off in shackles isn't likely to be available in the Public Room. It's more of a backroom deal that goes awry. As the above cases have proved, however, there are enough ethical people working in the securities industry to report wrongdoing when it's discovered. It doesn't matter if it's a stretch like the Martha Stewart case or a long-standing network like Kluger and Bauer, the truth will come out.

Individual investors have little to fear. Unless you have a buddy who's a top executive at a publicly traded company feeding you key, non-public information, you're not going to be doing anything illegal with insider trading. Follow trades reported to the SEC and you'll enjoy above-average market returns without doing anything shady, illegal, or that will result in fines and imprisonment.

With that in mind, let's look at how to decode the safe, legal insider trades that can help boost your investment returns and earn you a fortune.

3

Decoding Form 4

"Sunshine is the best disinfectant."

> — *Louis Brandeis, securities lawyer*
> *and US Supreme Court justice*

There are three key forms filed with the SEC that should interest investors looking to find out what insiders are up to. They're known as Forms 3, 4, and 5.

Form 3 is simply an insider's initial filing. This is filed when a company goes public and the CEO or CFO has to declare his or her initial stake in a now-public company.

Form 4 deals with changes in an insider's filings — whether the insider is buying or selling shares, and whether such trades are on the open market via buying and selling stock, or due to cashing in options.

Form 5 is filed when an individual ends his or her affiliation as an insider of a company. A retiring CEO, for example, or board of directors member whose term runs out, would file this form when he or she is no longer eligible to receive advanced information about a company. It's also filed for events that should have been reported earlier or were otherwise deferred.

Of these forms, Form 4 is the important one.

As you can see from the picture of Form 4, it's a pretty clear and organized document as far as government paperwork is concerned. Insiders have to list their name, the address of their company, and

FORM 4

FORM 4

☐ Check this box if no longer subject to Section 16. Form 4 or Form 5 obligations may continue. *See Instruction 1(b).*

UNITED STATES SECURITIES AND EXCHANGE COMMISSION
Washington, D.C. 20549

STATEMENT OF CHANGES IN BENEFICIAL OWNERSHIP

OMB APPROVAL
OMB Number: 3235-0287
Expires: December 31, 2014
Estimated average burden hours per response......0.5

(Print or Type Responses)

1. Name and Address of Reporting Person*			2. Issuer Name and Ticker or Trading Symbol		5. Relationship of Reporting Person(s) to Issuer (Check all applicable)
(Last)	(First)	(Middle)	3. Date of Earliest Transaction Required to be Reported (Month/Day/Year)	4. If Amendment, Date Original Filed(Month/Day/Year)	___Director ___10% Owner ___Officer (give title below) ___Other (specify below)
	(Street)				6. Individual or Joint/Group Filing (Check Applicable Line) ___Form filed by One Reporting Person ___Form filed by More than One Reporting Person
(City)	(State)	(Zip)			

Table I — Non-Derivative Securities Acquired, Disposed of, or Beneficially Owned

1. Title of Security (Instr. 3)	2. Transaction Date (Month/Day/Year)	2A. Deemed Execution Date, if any (Month/Day/Year)	3. Transaction Code (Instr. 8)		4. Securities Acquired (A) or Disposed of (D) (Instr. 3, 4 and 5)			5. Amount of Securities Beneficially Owned Following Reported Transaction (s) (Instr. 3 and 4)	6. Ownership Form: Direct (D) or Indirect (I) (Instr. 4)	7. Nature of Indirect Beneficial Ownership (Instr. 4)
			Code	V	Amount	(A) or (D)	Price			

mundane details like the ticker symbol, when the trade was made, how many shares traded and at what price, and the total value of the trade.

If only your tax form were this simple!

But, alas, the two-page form gets a bit more complex. Although the categories read in plain English, the reporting requirements have to conform to a code. Right beneath the name and address section on the left side of the first page, for example, reads:

1. Title of Security

(Instr. 3)

That's not the only code. Move three columns to the right, and under "Transaction Code (Instr. 8)," there are two small columns, one headed "Code" and the other headed "V." To the right, after "Amount," there's "(A) or (D)" under Column 4. The list goes on.

So what does it all mean? It's shorthand for various references listed on the website. Here's a table of all the codes:

General Transaction Codes

P — Open market or private purchase of non-derivative or derivative security

S — Open market or private sale of non-derivative or derivative security

V — Transaction voluntarily reported earlier than required, Rule 16b-3 Transaction Codes

A — Grant, award, or other acquisition pursuant to Rule 16b-3(d)

D — Disposition to the issuer of issuer equity securities pursuant to Rule 16b-3(e)

F — Payment of exercise price or tax liability by delivering or withholding securities incident to the receipt, exercise, or vesting of a security issued in accordance with Rule 16b-3

I — Discretionary transaction in accordance with Rule 16b-3(f) resulting in acquisition or disposition of issuer securities

M — Exercise or conversion of derivative security exempted pursuant to Rule 16b-3

Derivative Securities Codes (except for transactions exempted pursuant to Rule 16b-3)

C — Conversion of derivative security

E — Expiration of short derivative position

H — Expiration (or cancellation) of long derivative position with value received

O — Exercise of out-of-the-money derivative security

X — Exercise of in-the-money or at-the-money derivative security

Other Section 16(b) Exempt Transaction and Small Acquisition Codes (except for Rule 16b-3 codes above)

G — Bona fide gift

L — Small acquisition under Rule 16a-6

W — Acquisition or disposition by will or the laws of descent and distribution

Z — Deposit into or withdrawal from voting trust

Other Transaction Codes

J — Other acquisition or disposition (describe transaction)

K — Transaction in equity swap or instrument with similar characteristics

U — Disposition pursuant to a tender of shares in a change of control transaction

As you can see, it's a lot to take in. Most trades relate to an executive or director cashing in stock options, so they'd fall under the Derivative Securities Codes. Rule 16b-3 includes special situations.

Even with all these codes, investors looking through Form 4 filings can simply look for general transaction codes with a P or S. These indicate either a purchase or sale on the open market and weed out trades based on stock market options.

This gives us an idea of what insiders are doing with their actual cash. Are they putting their cash to work back in the business where they spend 40+ hours a week? Are they selling their existing stock position and getting out? Form 4 will let you know the key elements.

But being able to decipher a Form 4 to know that a trade occurred isn't enough. Investors need some context as well. What is the insider really doing? Let's take a look at some actual Form 4s to find out.

The Form 4 on page X is pretty straightforward. Here we see that Elon Musk bought shares of his company, Tesla Motors (TSLA), on

FORM 4 SHOWING TESLA MOTORS TRADE

FORM 4

☐ Check this box if no longer subject to Section 16. Form 4 or Form 5 obligations may continue. *See Instruction 1(b).*

(Print or Type Responses)

UNITED STATES SECURITIES AND EXCHANGE COMMISSION
Washington, D.C. 20549

STATEMENT OF CHANGES IN BENEFICIAL OWNERSHIP

OMB APPROVAL
OMB Number: 3235-0287
Expires: December 31, 2014
Estimated average burden hours per response. 0.5

1. Name and Address of Reporting Person* **Musk Elon**	2. Issuer Name and Ticker or Trading Symbol **TESLA MOTORS INC [TSLA]**	5. Relationship of Reporting Person(s) to Issuer (Check all applicable)

(Last) (First) (Middle)
3500 DEER CREEK ROAD
(Street)
PALO ALTO, CA 94304
(City) (State) (Zip)

3. Date of Earliest Transaction Required to be Reported (Month/Day/Year) **10/03/2012**

4. If Amendment, Date Original Filed(Month/Day/Year)

X Director   X 10% Owner
X Officer (give title below)   Other (specify below)
CEO

6. Individual or Joint/Group Filing (Check Applicable Line)
X Form filed by One Reporting Person
☐ Form filed by More than One Reporting Person

Table I — Non-Derivative Securities Acquired, Disposed of, or Beneficially Owned

1. Title of Security (Instr. 3)	2. Transaction Date (Month/Day/Year)	2A. Deemed Execution Date, if any (Month/Day/Year)	3. Transaction Code (Instr. 8) Code	V	4. Securities Acquired (A) or Disposed of (D) (Instr. 3, 4 and 5) Amount	(A) or (D)	Price	5. Amount of Securities Beneficially Owned Following Reported Transaction (s) (Instr. 3 and 4)	6. Ownership Form: Direct (D) or Indirect (I) (Instr. 4)	7. Nature of Indirect Beneficial Ownership (Instr. 4)
Common Stock	10/03/12		P(1)		35,398	A	$28.25	27,203,237	I	by Trust

October 3, 2012. In the top right corner, we can see that he's the CEO of the company, on the board of directors, and owns more than 10 percent of the company. That's an extremely bullish sign in an insider buy.

In the bottom row, we see that the purchase was common stock. Under Column 3 in the second row, we see that there's a P under the section "Code." We know from looking at the table of codes that that's a purchase. The V next to it means this information was filed voluntarily ahead of schedule. We can also see under the amount that this purchase was for 35,398 shares.

The Code A under Column 4, shows that the securities were acquired. That seems a bit redundant since we know there was an open-market purchase, but that's still pretty good for government paperwork.

Moving right, we see a price of $28.25 per share for this purchase of 35,398 shares. This may have been an average price over multiple trades, or it may have been one large trade at that price. We can see in the next column over that, as a result of this trade, Musk owned 27,203,237 shares when he filed the paperwork.

Finally, in the last two columns, we can see that these shares were bought indirectly, and that they're being held in a trust, rather than personally held by Musk.

Because Musk made an open market purchase here, he didn't even need to fill out anything in the next section on stock options. The second page simply relists his name, address, his insider relationship, and has his signature.

That's a pretty clear case of an insider buy on the stock market which investors can find out about in order to profit. Tesla Motors went on to become one of the best-performing stocks in 2013.

Let's take a look at a more common sight among Form 4 filings: an insider sale.

Consider the Form 4 data on page 28.

Here we see a trade by Warren Mitchell, a director at Clean Fuels Energy Corp (CLNE). Looking at the bottom part of the form, we can see that there are two lines showing common stock trades on October 1, 2013. The first line shows a Code M, which according to our decoding guide is the "exercise or conversion of derivative security exempted pursuant to Rule 16b-3."

FORM 4 SHOWING CLEAN ENERGY FUELS TRADE

FORM 4

UNITED STATES SECURITIES AND EXCHANGE COMMISSION
Washington, D.C. 20549

STATEMENT OF CHANGES IN BENEFICIAL OWNERSHIP

☐ Check this box if no longer subject to Section 16. Form 4 or Form 5 obligations may continue. *See Instruction 1(b).*

OMB APPROVAL
OMB Number: 3235-0287
Expires: December 31, 2014
Estimated average burden hours per response.... 0.5

(Print or Type Responses)

1. Name and Address of Reporting Person*	2. Issuer Name and Ticker or Trading Symbol	5. Relationship of Reporting Person(s) to Issuer
Mitchell Warren I	**Clean Energy Fuels Corp. [CLNE]**	(Check all applicable) X Director ___ 10% Owner ___ Officer (give title below) ___ Other (specify below)

(Last) (First) (Middle)	3. Date of Earliest Transaction Required to be Reported (Month/Day/Year)	4. If Amendment, Date Original Filed(Month/Day/Year)	
C/O CLEAN ENERGY FUELS CORP, 4675 MACARTHUR COURT, SUITE 800 (Street) **NEWPORT BEACH, CA 92660**	**10/01/2013**		6. Individual or Joint/Group Filing (Check Applicable Line) X Form filed by One Reporting Person ___ Form filed by More than One Reporting Person

| (City) (State) (Zip) |

Table I — Non-Derivative Securities Acquired, Disposed of, or Beneficially Owned

1. Title of Security (Instr. 3)	2. Transaction Date (Month/Day/Year)	2A. Deemed Execution Date, if any (Month/Day/Year)	3. Transaction Code (Instr. 8) Code	V	4. Securities Acquired (A) or Disposed of (D) (Instr. 3, 4 and 5) Amount	(A) or (D)	Price	5. Amount of Securities Beneficially Owned Following Reported Transaction (s) (Instr. 3 and 4)	6. Ownership Form: Direct (D) or Indirect (I) (Instr. 4)	7. Nature of Indirect Beneficial Owner- ship (Instr. 4)
Common Stock	10/01/13		M		3,000	A	$2.96	43,100	D	
Common Stock	10/01/13		S(1)		3,000	D	$13.5723	40,100	D	

In other words, he exercised a company stock option. In this case, we can see that Mr. Mitchell paid $2.96 per share for 3,000 shares of CLNE. He then turned around and, according to the S in the second line, sold those shares on the open market for an average price of $13.5723.

We can also see that by exercising the option, he increased his share position to 43,100, and then by selling 3,000 shares reduced it to 40,100. We can also see that these were shares he directly controlled. He didn't use a trust or exercise these options in the name of a family member.

Part 2 of Mitchell's trade simply reiterates that this trade involved derivatives and that he had a stock option with the right to

CLEAN ENERGY FUELS TRADE CONTINUED

FORM 4 (continued)

Table II — Derivative Securities Acquired, Disposed of, or Beneficially Owned
(*e.g.*, puts, calls, warrants, options, convertible securities)

1. Title of Derivative Security (Instr. 3)	2. Conversion or Exercise Price of Derivative Security	3. Transaction Date (Month/Day/Year)	3A. Deemed Execution Date, if any (Month/Day/Year)	4. Transaction Code (Instr. 8) Code	V	5. Number of Derivative Securities Acquired (A) or Disposed of (D) (Instr. 3, 4, and 5) (A)	(D)	6. Date Exercisable and Expiration Date (Month/Day/Year) Date Exercisable	Expiration Date	7. Title and Amount of Underlying Securities (Instr. 3 and 4) Title	Amount or Number of Shares	8. Price of Derivative Security (Instr. 5)	9. Number of derivative Securities Beneficially Owned Following Reported Transaction (s)(Instr. 4)	10. Ownership Form of Derivative Security: Direct (D) or Indirect (I) (Instr. 4)	11. Nature of Indirect Beneficial Ownership (Instr. 4)
Stock Options (Right To Buuy)	$2.96	10/1/13		M			3,000	(2)	5/5/15	Common Stock	3,000	$0	6,000	D	

Reporting Owners

Reporting Owner Name/Address	Relationships			
	Director	10% Owner	Officer	Other
Mitchel Warren I C/O CLEAN ENERGY FUELS CORP., 4675 MACARTHUR COURT, SUITE 800 NEWPORT BEACH, CA 92660	X			

buy at $2.96. From this second table, we can see that his options were good through May 5, 2015, and that the 3,000 shares were only one-third of the options he held, as he had 6,000 shares' worth of options remaining.

Of the two examples, the Clean Energy Fuels Corp. example is more representative of the average insider trade. But the insider trades that offer the best potential returns for investors to follow are more like the first example with Tesla Motors.

As with reading any document, there are a few key codes, and the guide in this chapter outlines every possible outcome. Now that we're equipped to read through all these forms, let's find a way to whittle this information down to the most important trades to follow in order to beat the stock market's average return.

4

Not All Insiders
Are Created Equal

"Get inside information from the president and you will lose half of your money. If you get it from the chairman of the board, you will lose all your money."

— *Jim Rogers*

S o far throughout this book, we've solely used the term "insiders." Yet this isn't some monolithic concept. Saying that an insider bought stock can have different investment implications depending on who is doing it, what that person's role is within a company (if any), and other factors, such as how much stock is bought.

That's because, among the various subgroups of insiders, there's a disproportionate amount of information that gets passed around. This thesis was first expounded in the classic article which appeared in Spring 1983 issue of the *Journal of Portfolio Management*, "Are Some Insiders More 'Inside' Than Others?"

The authors, Kenneth Nunn, Gerald Madden, and Michael Gombola, after looking at the data of insider trading based on various groups, concluded: "We hypothesize that an informational hierarchy exists, with access to non-public information and subsequent performance directly related to the insider's internal role."

In the usual dry, academic style that really sucks the fun out of reading the Journal of Portfolio Management, the authors conclude that there appears to be a slightly positive correlation between being atop the hierarchy of information and improved investment returns.

In other words, the more you know about a company, the better returns you'll get from buying and selling the stock. The higher up the insider who is disclosing the data is in that hierarchy, the more an individual investor should weigh the importance of the data.

Since not all insiders are created equal, with some performing even better than the average insider trader, a key way to find the best investment opportunities is to focus on trades being made by the best-performing groups. Investors could also avoid many of the potential losses that sometimes occur across individual insider trades by discounting trades made by the worst-performing groups. Let's look at the breakdown in further detail.

C-ream of the Crop: The C-Level Executives

Hopefully, a corporation's chief executive officer knows everything of material interest that's transpiring at his or her company. The CEO receives regular reports across the board, not only with regard to sales and production, but also with any accounting or legal concerns — the types of concerns that might not weigh on a stock's price for months or years.

As such, a CEO is at the peak of the corporate hierarchy. Not only does the CEO get the groundswell of daily information about a firm, he or she also has the ability to send new ideas down the

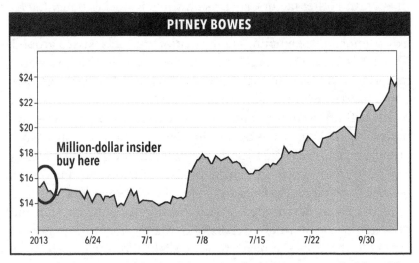

Pitney Bowes became one of the top-performing stocks of 2013. Investors who followed the CEO's million-dollar buy-in could have gone along for the wealth-building ride.

pipeline and make the key decisions of what changes, if any, the company needs to make.

For example, on May 7, 2013, Pitney Bowes (PBI) CEO Bradley Lautenback bought 66,000 shares at $15.36 per share, for a total value of $1,013,760. Within six months, shares had risen more than 54 percent, although most of that gain didn't happen overnight. Whatever the CEO was hearing from his employees day in and day out wasn't something that immediately boosted the share's prices. Investors had plenty of time to read through the Form 4 filings and get in on the trade.

Of course, the CEO isn't the only executive at the top of the chain. The Chief Financial Officer (CFO) also shares in most of the daily information, although he or she might not necessarily receive reports on every aspect of the company that the CEO does.

What's interesting about the CFO versus the CEO is that, as the key finance person, this officer may be better suited to interpreting the bottom-line results of a new policy being implemented, the latest sales figures, and so on.

Indeed, in a 2011 article in the *Journal of Financial and Quantitative Analysis* entitled "Are CFOs' Trades More Informative than CEOs' Trades?", Weimin Wang, Yong Chul Shin, and Bill Francis examine the differences in investment returns of these two high-level subgroups of insiders.

Since academic financial journal articles love raising questions in the headlines and then make you read 20-30 pages of dense jargon before arriving at a simple yes or no, I'll do you the courtesy of jumping straight to the conclusion. It's yes — the numbers guy performs better over time than the "big picture" guy.

"We find that CFOs earn statistically and economically higher abnormal returns following their purchases of company shares than CEOs. During 1992-2002, CFOs earned an average 12-month excess return that is 5% higher than that by CEOs. The superior performance by CFOs occurs notwithstanding controls for risk factors, and persists even after their trades are publicly disclosed. Further analysis shows that CFO purchases are associated with more positive future earnings surprises than CEO purchases, suggesting that CFOs incorporate better information about future earnings."

So CFOs tend to outperform CEOs, although both of these C-level executives do better than the average insider over time. Still, an extra 5 percent a year is nothing to scoff at, especially since it's an extra 5 percent tacked onto the already market-beating returns of the average CEO insider trade.

Following the general rule that multiple insiders buying are as valuable as the highest-ranking person making the trade, we can also conclude that if both the CEO and the CFO are buying shares (excluding exercising options), that's as bullish a sign as the just the CFO buying.

So when looking though SEC Form 4 filings, any direct buys by a corporation's CEO or CFO are absolutely worth a closer look.

Under the C-Level: The Board of Directors

The next key subgroup of insiders is the board of directors, which tends to meet at various times throughout the year, either in person or via conference call.

The directors aren't involved with the company's daily activities and might not have the most immediate knowledge of upcoming material events. But they are involved with approving long-term corporate strategies. They can approve or disapprove of a CEO's course of action. They are responsible for approving changes to dividend or share-buyback policies that may have an impact on share price.

Nevertheless, board members still pay close enough attention that they have a good idea as to the worth of the company at any given time. Directors also make up a larger group of people relative to key C-level employees, so there are plenty of opportunities to garner fast profits from their insider buys.

For instance, on October 10, 2013, Robert Walter bought 20,000 shares of Yum Brands (YUM). The parent company of Taco Bell, Pizza Hut, and KFC saw shares dive late in September due to concerns of a slowdown in the fast-growing China market. The 20,000 shares cost an average of $66.09 for a total buy-in of $1,321,799.

In short, despite getting less daily information, board members are very much in the flow of the corporate hierarchy. Some

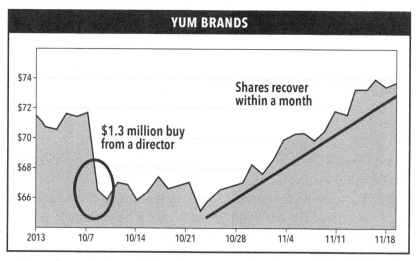

Directors have a good sense for when companies are undervalued, even if they don't have as much day-to-day information as a CEO or CFO. This insider buy in Yum Brands led to a 9.7 percent gain within six weeks, about what the stock market tends to return on average in a given year.

directors may be corporate officers. If so, then they tend to fall into the rank of a C-level executive.

That means that any insider trade they make will be listed on their Form 4 as an officer of the company *and* a board member, but the excess returns over time will fall under the C-level category.

The Blind Insiders: Big Money and Wall Street's Corporate Raiders

We all probably know at least one investor who's tried to put Warren Buffett's financial acumen to work without shelling out $170,000 for a share of Berkshire Hathaway. When Buffett makes new stock purchases in its portfolio, that information is updated quarterly by the SEC and disseminated. Many folks try to grab the coattails. And over time, that's a proven strategy.

But it's not insider trading.

When corporate raider Carl Icahn starts buying shares of a technology company hand over fist, demanding the return of excess cash on the books to shareholders via a higher dividend, that's a proven strategy . . . But it's not insider trading.

However, when Buffett or Icahn hit a 5 percent stake of a company, they have to disclose that information to the SEC immediately.

The form is a 13D, and it's the outsider equivalent of a Form 4. But that doesn't make them insiders, even though that's how the SEC treats them.

These money managers may end up having the largest single stake in the company and the chance to parade around on the news circuit, but they're not getting the daily information as C-level executives or getting to sit in on the long-term strategy sessions held by the board of directors.

Yet for all intents and purposes, they're treated as insiders by the SEC. But they're really not.

But a 5 percent stake in any company is a huge amount. Anyone with the capital and the willingness to take a large stake in a company probably has an idea based on public information that shares are undervalued.

Again, none of that is based on insider information. But smart investors like Buffett and Icahn have made a fortune buying undervalued shares without the help of being on the inside. That ties into their investment acumen, not any extra knowledge or inkling from closed-door meetings or the daily reports of company employees.

In some rare cases with corporate raiders like Icahn, the excess returns are a result of greenmail. That just means that, in exchange for selling their stake, corporate raiders get a higher return than the stock's current price. For money managers looking for a quick buck, a fast return can be more important than how the company is likely to fare operationally.

Other times, these players aren't so lucky. Carl Icahn's attempts to unlock greater value at Dell Computer before the company went private with Silver Lake Partners didn't lead to unlocking any value. Icahn's fight nearly brought shares to $15, but on the last day of trading, shares ended at $13.89.

The bottom line is simple. Despite being considered insiders, large shareholders who aren't on the board or working for the company have only the same idea of what's going on as the average investor. They just have much more money at stake that their views of the company's prospects are correct.

What can promote money managers and major shareholders to becoming real insiders (for the purposes of better investment returns, not the SEC definition) is a seat on the corporate board.

This is typically possible once someone amasses a 10 percent stake in a company.

Yes, the financial news will often have a breaking story on the latest buys and sells of Warren Buffett, Carl Icahn, and a host of other money managers. And for good reason — they're skilled, high-profile investors. But buying into a company doesn't make them insiders, even if they have to file information with the SEC. So for the sake of insider trading, unless something is happening along the lines of Buffett doubling down on a stock, focus instead on what corporate executives of a company are up to.

Also in this category are the more mundane players in the industry. An investment bank like Goldman Sachs might have a large stake in a company it recently helped with an initial public offering (IPO). It's normal for investment banks to retain some shares to sell later (or not). And these investment banks undoubtedly had all the financial information as insiders to help them prepare for their IPO. But, just like Buffett and Icahn, that doesn't make them key insider players worth following for the best source of profits.

Insurance companies and mutual funds are other prime examples. These firms may amass large stakes as well, but often these are held in a fiduciary relationship on behalf of their clients and as such have little relevance to be considered insider trades.

Most of these types of "insider" trades from major shareholders involve a Form 13D. Ignoring those filings with the SEC and focusing on Form 4 data will weed out a lot of the noise of insider trading so that you can focus on only the best insider opportunities.

Conclusion: Start at the Top of the Hierarchy and Work Your Way Down

The good news is that, despite all the different insider groups, insiders still collectively beat the market over time. But it's still important to recognize that not all insiders are created equal. Money managers are fundamentally outsiders, even when they have a 10 percent stake in the company.

Once they take a seat on the board of directors, they move up to a higher spot on the information hierarchy and as such get better returns. C-level executives have the best track record of insider trades, with financially-minded folks doing best.

When multiple insiders are buying around the same time (a cluster), the highest-level subgroup is where you're likely to get returns. So if a cluster of money managers are buying in, don't expect big things. If a few board of director members are buying, you should do better than the average insider trade. And if C-level executives are buying alongside a board member or major money manager, you should be golden.

At the end of the day, the best way to reduce your risk when investing alongside insiders is to look for direct buys from CEOs and CFOs and work down from there.

II

Beyond Insider Trading –
Other Factors to Look For

5

Technical Analysis

"The trend is your friend."

— Anonymous

So you've found a stock where multiple groups of insiders are bullish. Should you just dive right in? Proponents of investing alongside bullish insiders say yes. And if you do buy in immediately following reported insider trades, you should perform better than the market on average.

But some trades don't perform well. Insiders aren't omniscient. They may know a lot about their company. They may think their prospects for making money by buying the company stock is good. But sometimes, even they get it wrong.

For example, if you followed insider buying at Green Mountain Coffee Roasters (GMCR), you could have done extremely well. Back in August 2012, multiple insiders at the director level bought shares when they fell to the low $20 range.

As you can see from the Yahoo Finance chart on page 42, the buys came mostly in early August, yet insiders remained bullish as the share price rose from the $21 range to the $24 range — more than a 10 percent increase.

INSIDER BUYING AT GREEN MOUNTAIN COFFEE ROASTERS					
Aug 30, 2012	Moran, David E. Director	1,000	Direct	Purchase at $24.09 per share.	24,090
Aug 9, 2012	Wesley, Norman H. Director	5,000	Direct	Purchase at $23.75 - $24.5 per share.	121,000[2]
Aug 8, 2012	Wesley, Norman H. Director	5,000	Direct	Purchase at $24.39 - $25.04 per share.	124,000[2]
Aug 8, 2012	Geoffrion, Gerard Officer	5,000	Direct	Purchase at $23.34 per share.	116,700
Aug 6, 2012	Mardy, Michael J. Director	1,500	Direct	Purchase at $21.57 per share.	32,355

As many of these insiders later sold shares when they got into the $90 range, for profits as high as 328 percent, you might think that following insiders at GMCR would always lead to a profitable position.

Unfortunately, that's not the case.

On Aug 27, 2013, insider Susan Kilsby bought 1,500 shares of GMCR at $84.83 per share. Other insiders at the time were making automatic sales or exercising options, with SEC data showing more than 900,000 shares sold by directors and officers.

BUYS AND SELLS AT GREEN MOUNTAIN IN AUGUST 2013					
Aug 27, 2013	Kilsby, Susan S. Director	1,500	Direct	Purchase at $84.83 per share.	127,245
Aug 26, 2013	Moran, David E. Director	2,250	Direct	Automatic Sale at $88 per share.	198,000
Aug 26, 2013	Miller, Hinda Director	15,500	Direct	Option Exercise at $4.24 per share.	65,720
Aug 26, 2013	Miller, Hinda Director	15,500	Direct	Automatic Sale at $86.15 per share.	1,335,325
Aug 26, 2013	Kilsby, Susan S. Director	1,500	Direct	Purchase at $86.10 – $86.11 per share.	129,000[2]
Aug 26, 2013	Moran, David E. Director	2,250	Direct	Option Exercise at $1.52 per share.	3,420

Aug 20, 2013	Moran, David E. Director	4,000	Direct	Option Exercise at $4.24 per share.	6,080
Aug 20, 2013	Moran, David E. Director	4,000	Direct	Automatic Sale at $83 per share.	332,000
Aug 15, 2013	Moran, David K. Director	5,000	Direct	Purchase at $75.14 per share.	375,700
Aug 15, 2013	Moran, David K. Director	9,000	Indirect	Purchase at $75.14 per share.	676,260

Within two months, shares dropped like a rock due to concerns about the company's growth, sending them into the low $60s. Kilsby's position at that point was underwater by more than $32,000 on a $130,000 buy. This came after another buy Kilsby made the day before in the $86 range.

Bottom line: You don't need to buy immediately just because insiders are buying. You can wait a few days or even a few weeks while you do your homework and weed out. You have time, but not much.

According to H. Nejat Seyhun, author of *Investment Intelligence From Insider Trading*: "Within six months of the insider-trading month, about two-thirds of the stock-price reaction is completed. Subsequent price reaction during the next six months is smaller."

In other words, investors following insiders have a few weeks to jump into a trade after insiders do. That leaves time for us to look before we leap, so that we can avoid the insider trades that end up being financial pitfalls.

Fortunately, it doesn't take weeks or months to make sure a company's stock is already on the uptrend. Using what's known as a technical analysis, it can be done in a matter of minutes . . . if you know what to look for.

This is the key to winning or losing when following an insider trade. Why? Because technical analysis gives you clues as to the short-term market moves a stock, sector, or index is likely to make.

Since insider trades outperform over the short-term (less than a year), using technical analysis can help you filter out most of the insider trades that end up as losers. You can avoid the poor timing of the Susan Kilsbys of the insider world and invest with the winners instead.

I have found that you only need to use a few of the most basic and simple technical tools to weed through most of the poorer insider trades.

Technical Metrics to Consider With Insider Trades

Once you have a prospective company with insider buying on your radar, the first technical tool to look at is to simply pull up a one-year chart of the company on a site such as Google Finance or Yahoo Finance. Once you're there, you'll be able to pull down a tab that gives you the ability to look at a few technical analysis tools for free. I would suggest starting with *moving averages*.

A moving average is simply the average price of a stock over a specific time period. A 50-day moving average, for instance, would be the average closing price of a stock over the past 50 days. Every day, the newest price is added to the average and the oldest date is dropped, so it's a continually changing piece of data.

Typically, technical traders are bullish when a stock is trading above its moving average and bearish when a stock is trading below its moving average. Another major consideration is the direction the average is heading in over time.

I like to use both the 50-day and the 200-day moving averages. The purpose behind combining multiple moving averages is to get an idea for not only the current trend of the share price, but also when that's likely to change.

As you can see from the chart of Apple (AAPL) stock activity on page 45, in late 2012, the 50-day moving average dropped below the 200-day moving average. That's a bearish sign, and many technical traders used that as an opportunity to sell.

By spring 2013, the 50-day moving average of the stock stopped falling, indicating that the worst of the decline was over. Although shares started to rally in early summer, the most bullish sign came in September when the 50-day moving average crossed above the 200-day moving average.

Moving averages are about as simple as it gets, and they're widely used by enough traders that they continue to work after decades of use.

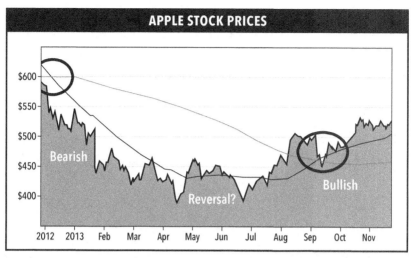

Based on moving averages, technical traders would have sold Apple stock in late 2012 and started buying in the summer or fall of 2013 as the moving averages moved closer before crossing.

But as you can see, using these moving averages work better over a longer period, i.e., months. There's another indicator that can give you more of a daily/weekly signal for when to invest (or not to invest) after a bullish insider.

This tool is called the **relative strength index**, or RSI. It measures the magnitude of gains over a given time period against the magnitude of losses. Without getting into the math, it uses an equation that ends up with a number between 1 and 100, with 50 as a neutral point.

Most technical analysts use a value of 30 or below to indicate an oversold stock likely to bounce, and a value of 70 or more to indicate an overbought stock likely to fall.

As with moving averages, this tool is available on any free financial site. It won't show up on a chart like the moving averages, but the historical RSI is usually shown under a stock chart for the corresponding period.

Looking at the RSI of Apple's stocks during the same time period, we find that there was an extremely oversold position in early March and late June.

Compared to the moving averages, these positions were close to the start and end of the reversal from the downward trend in Apple's share price to the upward trend.

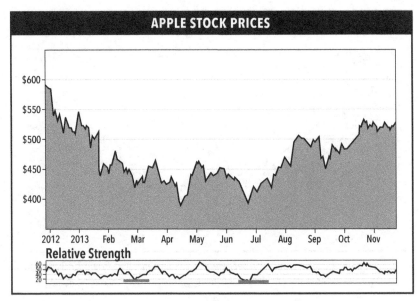

Apple's relative strength index showed multiple buying opportunities as the stock began to reverse its late 2012/early 2013 downtrend and rise in price again.

What makes this tool so useful with insider trading? As there's a tendency for all investments to revert to their mean, buying a stock that insiders have bought and which also registers a low RSI should lead to an immediate or near-immediate gain on a position.

A stock with an RSI in the middle range (40 to 60) isn't really showing a strong move and could go either way. If the *current middle range* is the result of moving up from an oversold range, it will probably continue to move up to overbought in the short term. If the trend has been declining, that's likely to continue too. This is simply because stocks fluctuate from overbought to oversold, so keeping an eye on this simple tool is an easy way to ensure that when you invest alongside an insider trade, you start to see immediate gains.

Technical Analysis is a Risk Reduction Tool for Entering Insider Trades

Hopefully, the two simple tools we've looked at should be more than enough to give you confidence that you're investing alongside insiders at the right time. After all, buying based solely on insider activity, while largely more profitable than index investing or throwing darts at the stock pages, still has its risks.

The technical tools here can also be used on broad market indices. If there's a downtrend there, you may want to hold off following an insider trade, as a broad market sell-off can send all shares down. Investing alongside insiders lost money in 2008. Yes, it still outperformed the market's 30 percent nosedive on a relative basis. *But it still lost money!*

What's more, even though insiders largely get it right, sometimes they do get it wrong. By avoiding the minority of insider trades that underperform the market, our returns are not only better, but we suffer fewer losses.

The bottom line? Insiders don't have perfect timing, although they have substantially better-than-average timing. Utilizing a few technical tools, we can reduce the possibility of investing alongside insiders at the wrong time.

These technical tools work best for figuring out when to enter an insider trade (and possibly when to exit an insider trade as well). For a longer-term view of what may happen to shares over the next six to twelve months, let's look beyond these indicators and toward fundamental analysis for some clues.

6

Fundamental Analysis

"The underlying principles of sound investment should not alter from decade to decade, but the application of these principles must be adapted to significant changes in the financial mechanisms and climate."

— *Ben Graham*

As noted in earlier chapters, insiders buy in with their own money for one reason and one reason only: They expect shares to trade higher.

But *why* do they expect shares to go higher? That's a question that often goes unanswered. Insiders only have to disclose that they made a trade, not their motivation for doing so. Many analysts who look into the matter try to assign some kind of reason.

In the last chapter, we looked at technical reasons for insiders to buy their shares. In this chapter, we'll look at fundamental factors that may explain why insiders are bullish. As with technical indicators, fundamental indicators can be used to weed out potentially poor trades. But, as always, when investing alongside insiders, the important thing is the insider buy, not any technical or fundamental indicator.

So what's fundamental analysis? It's looking at a company's underlying business, cash flows, growth, and the like to determine the company's true value. That value may be significantly higher or lower than the current share price on the market. If it's lower, analysts will either sell shares short or simply not own them. If the fundamental value is significantly higher than the current share price, shares are worth owning.

For example, a company trading at $20 per share with 10 percent revenue growth and $15 per share in cash would be considered a bargain by fundamental analysts. But a company trading at $200 per share that isn't earning any money yet — isn't seeing any revenue growth with $20 per share in debt, may not be worth buying on a fundamental level.

When it comes to insider trading, there are a few fundamental factors that can be used as a "gut check" to find the best potential opportunities.

Of course, it's important to remember that fundamental analysis takes a long-term view; a company that's undervalued may have to wait years for the market to realize its mistake and allow it to trade at a higher price. The benefits of insider trading take place over a shorter time period, but insiders themselves are sometimes unable to trade their stock over the short term given the issue of lockout periods.

A lockout period is simply a time before or after a major announcement, such as quarterly earnings, where insiders can't buy or sell shares. This prevents insiders from trying to time the market with their own company's shares. The lockout period is set by the company's own trading standards, so some firms have stringent standards and some have none. The only time the SEC gets involved with a lockout period is when a company first goes public, and insiders aren't allowed to sell their now-public shares for a pre-determined period.

So, compared to technical analysis, fundamental analysis doesn't have as much of a play in the world of insider trading, but it can still be useful if you're using insider buying as a tool to narrow down investment positions for your own portfolio.

I've found that by looking at a few key fundamental indicators, one can get a good ballpark estimate for a company's valuation that sufficiently explains why insiders are bullish. Let's take a look at each in more detail.

Valuation Metrics for Insider Trades

VALUATION METRIC NO. 1: REVENUE GROWTH

Revenue growth (year over year) is a simple and effective way of looking at a company's growth prospects. A company that's growing revenue consistently over time should see higher earnings per share, and in turn a higher share price. If a company's revenue is experiencing higher-than-average growth, then the shorter-term performance could be even better.

I like looking at revenue better than earnings with an insider buy. That's because revenue looks at the actual cash coming in before all sorts of accounting changes that can turn profits into losses and vice versa.

What I'm looking for in a company with insider buying is revenue growth in the 10 percent or higher range. Anything less isn't a clear fundamental signal. Revenue growth is a good "big picture" look at a company's financial prospects. It also ties in with the next key item to look at: return on equity.

VALUATION METRIC NO. 2: RETURN ON EQUITY

How effective is the company at using its money to make more money? That's what this metric, return on equity (ROE), tells us. A high ROE is better than a low one, especially for a company that's been labeled as a growth play.

A company's ability to earn $1.50 for every dollar it spends will grow substantially faster and better over time than a company that earns only $1.10 for every dollar it spends. So, when it comes to looking at profit margins and ROE, the higher the number, the better.

A company with a high ROE offers investors a way to invest defensively in an increasingly commoditized world. Many small, niche companies have high profit margins, but they can't grow because of their niche.

That's where return on equity comes in. A company that can generate high amounts of cash and continually reinvest can sustain a path of high earnings growth over time. Eventually, this will be reflected in higher share prices. Anyone who has owned shares of Apple in the past 10 years can attest to this fact, as the company reinvested its profits from the iPod into other products like the iPhone and iPad.

More importantly, companies with consistently high profit margins or ROE often have a reason for doing so. This may include a powerful brand, technology, a large portfolio of patents, or some other factor that creates a veritable "moat" around earnings.

Looking at profit margins and ROE over time gives you a way to essentially identify likely moats without having to look at the minutiae of a company's assets.

It's little wonder, then, that ROE is one of the most important metrics you can use for assessing a prospective investment.

VALUATION METRIC NO. 3: PROFIT MARGINS

Similar to ROE, a company's basic profit margins can be a key way of looking at a company. But it's more defensive than ROE. Many firms operate in a niche. The products or services they offer are ultra-specific, and as such, may not have huge growth prospects, even if they're earning money hand over fist. Seeing their sector double or triple in value is unlikely. So finding the most profitable company in a small part of the market can have a huge advantage over time.

That's why profit margins are a great metric. Smaller firms with insiders buying should show high profit margins, but not necessarily high ROE. What's more, insiders at smaller firms likely have a much better eye on how their competitors (if any) are faring. So insider buys at small companies with high profit margins tend to do better than the average insider trade over time.

Companies with consistently high profit margins typically have some kind of competitive advantage, so insider buying at a company with high profit margins should be a no-brainer trade. The part that requires a bit of digging, however, is figuring out whether a company has high profit margins but a low return on equity because of its being in a niche.

Combined with insider trades, companies with profit margins of at least 10 percent for commoditized industries like mining, manufacturing, or food production is a good cutting-off point. For more technology-based firms or more innovative products and services, a 25 percent or greater profit margin makes a good point for whittling down insider investment opportunities.

Other Valuation Metrics: Things to Look For

The above measures should cover the most basic, necessary, fundamental-analysis metrics when combined with insider trading. There are a few other factors you might want to consider, particularly if you're looking less at trading alongside insiders and more at using insider trading as a jumping-off point for building a long-term investment portfolio.

- **Enterprise value/earnings before interest, taxes, deductions, and amortization (EV/EBITDA).** This ratio looks at the total value of a company (market cap of the stock + outstanding debt), divided by its earnings before accounting changes. It's a little more substantive than the price/earnings ratio, since this includes a company's total debt in the picture, which can weigh on a company but not necessarily affect the stock's price.

- **Dividend and dividend growth.** Many firms with insider buying pay a dividend. If that dividend is growing, and insiders suspect that it is likely to increase further over time, this may play a role in buying shares. This occurred in 2013 with shares of Equal Energy (EQU). Multiple insiders bought shares around the time the company reinstated its dividend. Investors who buy shares of companies with growing dividends typically see share prices increase as well.

- **Status of a company's other competitors.** Sometimes, a company might not be doing well but its competitors may be even worse off. In the past decade, this has been seen most apparently with the consolidation in the retail industry. Best Buy wasn't doing well during the financial crisis, but it fared better than Circuit City. Barnes and Noble survived when competing- bookseller Borders failed. If insiders are buying and there doesn't seem to be a good technical or fundamental reason, looking at the performance of competitors may give a good clue.

Essentially, insiders do buy their company's stock when they see that the fundamentals look good. But more often it's because there will be a trigger event in the near future . . . like beating earnings, a breakout product, a buyout offer from a competitor, or some other favorable news item.

Remember, insider trading is neither technical nor fundamental. It's a different signal entirely. Therefore, technical and fundamental factors should just be used as a means of weighing the possibility that a specific insider trade will work out better than the average trade. By combining these tools with an insider trade, investors can reduce the probability of getting into trades that lose money. Over time, not losing money with investments is more powerful than scoring large gains. A 50 percent loss in a stock, for instance, will need to double in value just to get back to breakeven!

Technical analysis is better for trades lasting a few days or weeks, whereas fundamental analysis will work better for following insider trades over a period of weeks to months.

7

The Utility of Insider Sales

"Insider selling was the trigger but not the main driving force."
— *Sir John Templeton, on why he*
shorted tech stocks in early 2000

Throughout this book, we've looked largely at insider sales. That's because most insiders acquire stock options, so selling isn't *necessarily* an indicator that investors should be selling their shares too. Most insider transactions involve acquiring company stock via options and either retaining the shares or selling them. Indeed, the SEC data will sometimes indicate when a sale was planned in advance by the insider.

The motives for selling stock are the same as your motives for taking your paycheck and saving a little, spending a little, and investing a little. In September 2013, for instance, Best Buy went out of its way to explain the $10.4 million share sale by CEO Hubert Joly — he needed the cash to finish his divorce settlement.

Most of the time, as with insider buying, a selling insider won't disclose the exact reason for a sale. That's fine, as the important thing to bear in mind with insider sales is that it really doesn't affect the stock's subsequent performance, except under certain specific conditions.

Indeed, insider selling is so prevalent that, on average, insiders will sell more than 25 shares for every share bought by an insider.

The chart on page 56 looks at the sell/buy ratio of insiders for a two-year period from mid-2011 through mid-2013. There are huge

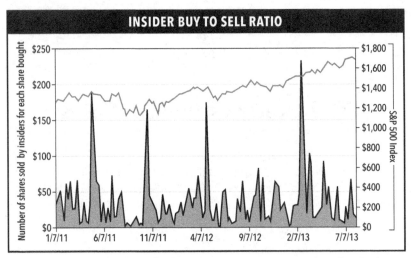

INSIDER BUY TO SELL RATIO

Insider sales always beat insider buys by a huge factor, with some spikes of 150+ shares sold for every share bought by an insider. That's why insider buys are a clearer buy signal than insider sales are for selling.

spikes of insiders selling shares, even as the stock market continued to rise. That's a sign that insiders needed to diversify (and possibly thought that their shares were overvalued), even if there was more upside potential.

However, there are times when insider selling *is* a sign that a stock might be trending down. In that case, it's important to recognize the signs.

The biggest sign to be aware of is when large clusters of insiders are selling shares. It doesn't matter if they're existing shares that the insiders have owned for years or if they're newly acquired shares via maturing stock options. When multiple insiders are selling around the same time, it's the closest you'll get to a red flag that a company's share price might be headed down.

It's how the great value investor Sir John Templeton amassed what he called "the easiest money" he ever made. In 2000, he shorted IPO tech stocks that were coming out of their lockup period. Templeton instinctively knew that most insiders at these tech companies would dump their shares on the market the instant it was legally permissible for them to do so. Many of these tech-bubble firms had no earnings or revenue, and had often posted triple-digit gains following their IPO, thanks to the mania of the time.

By shorting a basket of stocks right before the lockout period expired, Templeton made nearly $100 million in less than six months. Sir John was 88 years old and officially "retired" at the time.

That's telling on a smaller scale. When insiders are working in lockstep to dump their shares on the open market, it's a sign that you should sell shares if you own them. While you don't need to sell shares short like Templeton did at the height of the tech-stock bubble, at the very least, it's a sign that there are better investment opportunities elsewhere.

If an insider is departing and no longer has an insider relationship, he or she will file a Form 5 with the SEC to end the mandatory disclosure requirements. But typically former insiders won't immediately sell their shares right away, and will likely retain some stake after they're no longer considered insiders.

Bottom line: Insiders are so well compensated with corporate shares these days that insider selling is rarely as good a signal to sell as insider buying is to buy. What does matter is when multiple insiders are dumping their shares on the open market.

8

The Money Multiplier System

"Give me a lever long enough and a fulcrum on which to place it, and I shall move the world."

— Archimedes

Throughout this guide, we've looked at investment returns strictly based on how shares have performed after insiders have traded them. On the whole, investing with insiders beats the market. Investing strictly on CEO buys or multiple insider buys does even better. Holding those investments for three to six months captures most of the above-average gain, which lasts for about a year after the initial buy.

With that short of a time frame in mind, there's a fantastic investment tool that can be used to improve your returns. It can turn 20 percent gains into 40 percent gains or higher. It could even be used to put cash in your pocket when insiders get bullish instead. As well, it can allow you to take larger positions with less capital.

That tool is stock options, and the SEC requires that the same form be filed for options trading just as with stock trading.

Yes, stock options are a form of leverage. As such, they can be risky. But that's only true if investors don't use options responsibly. Buying 100 options for a few dollars in the hope that you can sell them when they double is an extremely risky proposition, as each option contract controls 100 shares of stock, which means you're playing with 10,000 shares, the market price of which might exceed your overall portfolio!

However, when used with lower-risk trades, options can provide the right mix of leverage and/or, a reduced capital outlay. Either way, that helps boost your returns even further when investing based on insider trades.

Let's start by reviewing how options work, and how call and put options can be used to multiply your wealth. If you're already familiar with how options work, and are set up to trade options, you can skip this next section.

Options 101

First thing's first: An option is a contract to buy or sell a specific financial product, known as the option's *underlying instrument*. For equity options, the underlying instrument is a stock. A McDonald's option relates to McDonald's stock; an Apple option relates to Apple stock; a SPY option relates to the SPDR S&P 500 ETF, and so on.

The contract itself establishes a specific price, called the strike price, at which the contract may be exercised. And it has an expiration date. When an option expires, it no longer has value and no longer exists.

Standardized options contracts have been around since 1973 and are increasingly popular with investors. More than 3 billion contracts are traded annually in the United States. The popularity of options lies in the fact that they give traders flexibility, reduce and limit risk, and offer high potential returns.

To understand options, we can start by thinking about buying an option on a house. In fact, many commercial real estate deals do involve options.

In our example, suppose you want to buy a home for $500,000 within three months (option expiration).

In exchange for this option to buy, you pay the seller 5 percent or $25,000, an amount referred to as the premium. Two weeks later, you learn that a nearby airport is going to expand its runways and will be purchasing all of the surrounding property, including your new home, for 50 percent over market value.

Because you have an option to buy at $500,000, your purchase price is locked in. Your new home just went from being worth $500,000 to $750,000. By exercising the option and then flipping the house to the airport, you have just realized a $250,000 profit.

On the other hand, say over that same time period you discover that the home is infested with termites and is structurally unsound, needing $300,000 in repairs. Your new house just went from a dream home to a money pit. Because you have an option to buy, not an obligation, you can walk away from the contract, losing your $25,000 premium payment but saving yourself from $275,000 in repairs.

The above example is a call option. Remember, options come in two varieties — *calls* and *puts* — and you can buy or sell either type. You make those choices — whether to buy or sell and whether to choose a call or a put — based on what you want to achieve as an options investor.

Because an option buyer can pay a relatively small premium for market exposure in relation to the contract value (usually 100 shares of the underlying stock), an option is a form of leverage.

An investor can see large-percentage gains from comparatively small, favorable-percentage moves in the underlying index.

Leverage also has downside implications. If the underlying stock price does not rise or fall as anticipated during the lifetime of the option, leverage can magnify the investment's percentage loss.

Options offer their buyers a predetermined, set risk. However, if the owner's options expire with no value, this loss is limited to the amount of the premium paid for the option. You cannot lose more than what you paid in, and in theory, your upside is unlimited.

It can look a little confusing if you go onto financial websites and look at options, as they just look like a string of letters and numbers. Let's go through an option and see what each part represents.

Say you see a string of numbers, letters, and words that looks like this: **MCD130119C9000**

The first part is the ticker symbol for the underlying stock the option is based on. In this example, it's McDonald's. The six numbers after the ticker symbol, 130119, represent the expiration date of the option — January 19, 2013.

The C indicates that this is a call option, which gives buyers the right, but not the obligation, to buy shares of McDonald's at any time between now and the expiration.

Finally, the 9000 represents the strike price, which in this case is $90 per share.

One more thing to remember: Every options contract is for 100 shares of stock. So in this example, exercising the options would require the buyer to buy 100 shares of McDonald's at $90, for a total cost of $9,000.

Most options are what's known as "American style." These options can be re-traded before their expiration date. This means you can put on an options trade, and, if conditions dramatically change, you can get out of the position immediately rather than having to sit around and potentially wait weeks or months for the options to expire.

Investors interested in getting started with options should contact their broker to ensure they're already able to do so. If not, getting prepared to trade options is a simple process. It typically requires additional paperwork and can take a few days to clear.

There are four levels of options trading that you can set. For most investors, level 2 provides the ability to buy call and put options, which works for most trades, particularly those alongside insiders. For more advanced traders, or those who want to invest with options for income, level 4 allows the full range of options strategies, including a more advanced strategy for generating income from insider trades that we'll look at further below.

With those basics of what options are and how they work, let's look at how they can be used to magnify the profits from insider trades, starting with the simplest options trade of all: the purchase of a call option.

Call Options and Insider Trades: Magnifying Gains

Most investors dipping their toe into the options pond will want to stick with call options. That's because they're better understood than put options, and because the advantages of insider trading boil down to higher stock prices, which make call options more appropriate to use.

As stated above, buying a call option gives the buyer the right, but not the obligation, to buy 100 shares of a stock (stock being the underlying instrument) at a specific price (the strike price) up to a specific date (the strike date). If the price of the stock goes up, the option can go up much higher — as much as 5 to 10 times. That depends on a variety of factors. An option with a strike price well above the current price won't move as far as a call option with a strike price right where the stock is trading.

An option further from its expiration will trade at a higher price, reflecting the added time premium; and with a higher price, a $1 move in that option won't have as high a percentage move as a $1 move in an option at a lower strike price. As the option ticks closer to expiration, however, this time premium will disappear, so investors looking to use options over long periods of time should be aware of how much that premium is before they buy.

With that in mind, investors can either buy very out-of-the money options for pennies. In this scenario, these options have a low likelihood of being worth anything at the expiration date, but they could trade in large percentage gaps upward and offer triple-digit returns.

Alternatively, investors could buy contracts with a strike price just slightly above the underlying stock's current price. This has a higher likelihood of being worth more if the stock rises and consequently will trade higher.

Which situation is best when trading based on insider moves? It can depend. For the most part, going slightly above the current strike price makes the most sense, even if the total percentage returns end up lower. And that's OK because the key to using options with insider trading is to maximize the statistical advantage that insider buying provides.

Remember, not all insider trades will be successful. In an extremely bad year for stocks, even trading alongside insiders could lead to losses. So sticking to options with a strike price close to the stock's current price is the way to go. Let's look at an example.

CALL OPTION OPPORTUNITY NO. 1: TRIPLE-DIGIT GAINS IN A SIDEWAYS-TRADING STOCK

For example, Western Gas Partners (WES) insiders reported bullish buying in May of 2013, also following insider buying in December of 2012. Although this energy producer is structured as an MLP, there were also call options to trade.

With the share price near $60, you could have done well buying call options a few months out, such as the November 2013, $60 calls. Within two weeks after the most recent insider trades were

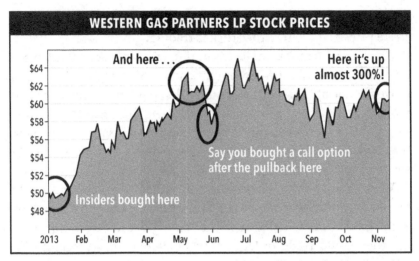

WESTERN GAS PARTNERS LP STOCK PRICES

And here . . .

Here it's up almost 300%!

$64
$62
$60
$58
$56
$54
$52
$50
$48

Say you bought a call option after the pullback here

Insiders bought here

2013 Feb Mar Apr May Jun Jul Aug Sep Oct Nov

Following a cluster of insider buys and a near-immediate pullback can lead to tremendous profits, especially with the use of call options to make a bullish bet.

disclosed, shares of WES pulled back, providing the opportunity to buy the November $60 calls around $0.45.

What happened next? The chart shows a trading pattern of the stock going up (hitting 52-week highs), followed by a decline that took it once again below the latest insider buying point.

Even if you didn't cash out right away, the options went to $1.70 at expiration. Based on the option entry point of around $0.45, you would have made gains of 277 percent! That's what I did with this stock, turning a trade on a range-bound stock into an opportunity to collect a triple-digit gain.

That's the power of options in a portfolio. The trade-off, however, is that these larger percentage returns are typically done with less money at stake. Buying one WES call option would have cost you less than $50 for the 100 share contract, whereas buying 100 shares would have set you back more than $5,500.

The other great advantage of call options is that, in this case, I didn't have to buy shares of an MLP (master limited partnership). Although I like them for the long term, trading in and out of MLPs can be a headache during tax season because they require extra paperwork.

By using options and reselling them later without exercising them, I managed to avoid this extra work and expense on my tax returns. Since options trade on a variety of instruments from ETFs and REITs to MLPs, there can be similar advantages from a tax perspective as well.

That's a classic example of using *at-the-money options* (an option with a strike price that is identical to the price of the underlying instrument) to earn high returns when following insider trades. But as I mentioned above, you can also use options with higher strike prices — that are further *out-of-the-money* — to generate high returns as well.

CALL OPTION OPPORTUNITY NO. 2: GENERATING DOUBLE-DIGIT RETURNS IN A STOCK THE MARKET HATES

I was a bit surprised to see some insider buying in PulteGroup (PHM) in late July and early August of 2013. A trio of directors — a *cluster* — bought nearly $500,000 in shares.

The real estate market, and more specifically the homebuilder sector, was giving off a lot of contrary signals to both value and technical investors at the time. Shares of Pulte had been in a decline — from the mid-$20s a few months earlier into the high teens. It seemed the insiders were looking at a potential rebound to make some relatively quick profits. I wasn't entirely convinced. But the insider buying was large enough in scope to convince me to put out a trade with a smaller capital outlay.

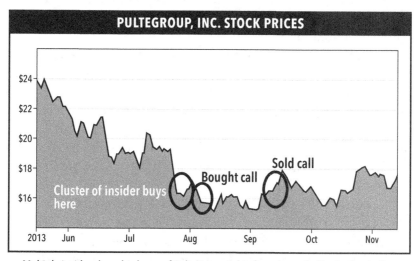

Multiple insiders bought shares of PulteGroup right after a large decline in share price. Although shares have started to recover, options traders could have performed better, even as the stock reached a short-term bottom a month after the insider buys.

So, in order to limit my risk, I used a far out-of-the-money option to see if these insiders had indeed found a great buying price for their shares, buying the January 20 call option for $0.74 on July 30, 2013.

The chart on Pulte shows that insiders were a bit early, but also relatively close to the stock's bottom over the last half of 2013.

The move wasn't huge, but even with the gyrations of the stock, investors who bought the call option would have seen some swings between profit and loss before being able to lock in a modest profit on September 16 for a 14.86 percent gain.

Advanced Options Strategies for Insider Trading: Cash in on Puts

Call options make the most sense for insider trades because such trades historically rise in value. However, there's another way to use options that allow you to safely generate income as well. It involves put options. But rather than buying, investors will go in and *sell* put options instead.

It sounds somewhat unusual, and it's a bit roundabout. When you sell a put option, you're basically saying, "Pay me money now, and if your stock goes below this price on this date, I'll buy it." It's a way of getting paid to wait for cheaper prices and is a great tool for building up stock positions. Rather than waiting for a pullback and sitting in cash, you're already committed and getting paid the option premium for doing so.

This strategy, whether used with insider trading or not, puts a different statistical edge on your side. The majority of stock options tend to expire worthless. The bets simply don't pay off. By selling options, you're putting that edge to work. When you sell an option, over time, it loses time premium. So, even if you buy back a put option to close out your position later, you can still make money thanks to the loss in premium. If the underlying stock rises in price, the option will also lose value.

Of course, you can also hold the option until the strike date and see it expire worthless, in which case you'll get to keep *all* the money you received from selling the put option in the first place.

Here's where it gets good. When combining this strategy with insider trading, you get the advantage of both statistical edges. Because bullish insiders greatly increase the chances of a stock going up over the next year (and really only over the next year), selling put options when insiders are bullish can immediately put money in your pockets, with a high likelihood of getting to keep the entire premium.

Let's take a look at another example where I've put cash into my portfolio immediately by using this strategy.

PUT SELLING OPPORTUNITY NO. 1: IMMEDIATE CASH FROM A GLOBAL CONSULTING POWERHOUSE

On July 2, 2013, Stephen Rohleder, an officer at British-based Accenture, bought nearly $1.5 million of his company's stock at $71.99 per share. Although the company is based in the UK, it trades on the New York Stock Exchange, which means it's subject to the same reporting requirements for insiders as any US company.

As a large-cap company with a global reach and plenty of insiders, there is a lot of insider activity. Mostly, it involves acquiring options and exercising them, as well as automatic sales of accumulated positions. So finding a huge buy amid all the regular selling was a good signal that shares might have some more upside here, but not necessarily as much as if there were more insiders.

Of course, there was another factor as well. In June, shares of the firm fell sharply as it drastically reduced its outlook for the rest of the year, including a reduced revenue forecast.

Following a devastating drop on a lower financial outlook, one insider put nearly $1.5 million to work in the company's stock. It's been a bit of a roller coaster, but profitable.

So in this case, with a large-cap global company seeing a large insider buy, selling a put option against it made the most sense as a way to profit. I sold a January 2014, $65 put option on ACN for $2.05, or $205. The $65 strike gave me some downside protection. If the stock was at, say, $66 in January, I could still have made money by selling the put option, but would be sitting on a loss had I bought the stock.

Following the drop and the insider buy, shares began to recover . . . and then fall again . . . and then recover. Although the stock went on to evenlower lows in August and October, it only briefly dipped below $70. Following that, shares recovered more than half of their steep June drop, and as of the end of 2013. The put option traded for $0.20, but expired at zero in January.

PUT SELLING OPPORTUNITY NO. 2: INSIDERS MADE A $30 MILLION BUY-IN

In September 2013, Kevin Kaiser, a 26-year-old analyst at the research firm Hedgeye Risk Management, called out blue-chip oil and gas pipeline company Kinder Morgan (KMI). In his opening shot, he went to Twitter, where he proclaimed that that the company was "a house of cards, completely misunderstood and mispriced."

Before the specifics could come out, that was sufficient to spook the market into sending shares nearly 6 percent lower.

But the subsequent report, which outlined issues concerning the interrelation of the company's various subsidiaries and operating firms, was a dud. Yes, the master limited partnership (MLP) structure was a bit unusual compared to other companies. But it was a time-tested model of delivering shareholder value. I even pointed out at the time that this successful company is the best thing to come out of Enron, given the fact that its original founders and assets were spun out of the defunct energy giant.

The report wasn't enough to send shares back to their pre-jitter heights, but the more experienced members of the MLP were quick to look into its shortcomings and even noted that there was now a buying opportunity in Kinder Morgan.

Enter Richard Kinder, founder of the company. He stepped in and bought 500,000 shares of the management company, KMI, at $35.74. That's a buy-in of $17.87 million dollars. And that wasn't the first time he bought shares. He bought another 500,000 shares in June at $35.78 each.

Kinder wasn't the only insider either. Company director Fayez Sarofim bought more than $10.6 million in shares on August 9 and over $4.4 million in shares on August 8. In the space of a month, insiders had bought more than $30 million in shares. Over a 3 month period, it was closer to $50 million.

I liked what I saw about the company, but I already own shares of the MLP, Kinder Morgan Partners (KMP), in my investment portfolio. The buying was concentrated in the management company, Kinder Morgan Inc. (KMI), which pays a lower dividend and doesn't have the tax advantages that an MLP does.

With that in mind, I sold KMI put options, specifically those valued at $32.50 on March 2014. I sold them at $1.40 each. Although the option hasn't had a chance to expire as I write this, it's well on its way. That's because the stock has range-traded since September, with shares up about 1 percent since the last major buy-in by Richard Kinder. However, were I to close these options out as I write this, I would only have to pay about 70 percent of what I bought the options for.

That illustrates the power of selling put options on a stock that trades flat or in a narrow range. Your returns can be better than simply buying the stock. If the stock takes off, however, you'll still make money.

Bringing It All Together: Which Options Strategy Is Best?

So what strategy is best when placing options trades based on insider trading? I've found that buying calls works better with smaller-cap companies (provided they have options). The percentage gains on smaller-cap companies tend to exceed those of mid- or large-cap companies within 12 months from the start of insider buys, and using an option can help magnify that return even more.

Because smaller-cap companies tend to be more volatile and have higher risk, it's also reassuring to know that the most money you can lose is your option premium, which is far less money at stake than going out and buying shares.

For selling put options as a strategy, the lower volatility of larger companies makes it a better place. Lower volatility means less chance of a downside, but also lower potential total returns. For large-cap companies, I like to look for options three to six months out, where the bulk of the gain from the insider trade tends to occur. I also like to look for options that give me a 3-5 percent return on my cash.

So for a stock selling at $50, I would look for an option to sell where I could get at least $1.50 or higher ($150 divided by $5,000 is 3 percent). For most large-cap stocks, that's also a cash return on par or in excess of the annual dividend in half the time.

Also, it's important to remember that options, while a powerful tool to boost returns, aren't always available on many companies. Even smaller companies that do have some options to trade might not have the liquidity necessary to guarantee you can get out of the trade when you need to.

I've found that I can get sufficient liquidity if the option has at least 100 contracts already outstanding for every one option that I want to trade.

Investors should never forget that options have risks akin to investing in penny stocks. They can have high spreads between the *bid* (what someone is willing to buy an option for) and the *ask* (what someone is willing to sell for). While you can generally get into an options trade at the midpoint between those two prices, that isn't always the case. The spread may be too wide for anyone willing to budge. There might not be enough liquidity to make sizeable trades at that price point either. If you want to trade 10 options, find a contract with more liquidity.

Finally, bear in mind that these are just a few things that I've learned from actually putting money to work by trading options based on insider buying. They're rules that work in today's market environment, but which might not work forever. But when it comes to insider trading, owning the stock is sometimes the better choice. In the case of some companies, it's the *only* choice. That's why these money multiplier strategies are powerful — their availability is limited.

Conclusion: The 10 Key Takeaways From This Guide

"The minute you get away from the fundamentals — whether it's proper technique, work ethic, or mental preparation — the bottom can fall out of your game."

— *Michael Jordan*

Throughout this guide, we've looked at the power of insider trading. It's mostly a boring, clockwork routine of insiders acquiring stock options and then selling them. But when they buy their shares instead, it's a powerful signal that can help generate significant, above-average investment returns over time. What's more, you may be able to do even better by using insider trades as a jumping-off point to whittle trades down to those with the best chance of outperforming the market. This data is available for anyone willing to filter through the government paperwork filed with the SEC.

With all of the concepts we've looked at with insider trading, the key factors to bear in mind can be expressed as follows.

1. **Open-market trades are the most important factor.** Options-related trades do not correlate with higher (or lower) stock prices.

2. **Purchases signal the best buying opportunities.** Some insider sales will fall under open-market trades. Purchases — particularly open-market, insider purchases — provide the best opportunity.

3. **Size matters!** A single trade for 100 shares doesn't indicate a firm conviction in a company's future. Buying thousands of shares, however, does. Typically, the more an insider buys, the better a stock will do over the next 12 months. This extra gain based on increased insider buying peaks when insiders buy around $1 million worth of shares.

4. **Hierarchy matters.** Buys from CEOs and CFOs perform better on average than buys from members of the board of directors. Major institutional holders are, for all intents and purposes, outsiders.

5. **Clusters of insider buying are better than single buys.** Following the herd of insiders is a much better signal than a "lone wolf" who might be mistaken.

6. **Insider buys are neither technical nor fundamental factors.** While those factors are worth double-checking to avoid potential losses, insider buying is a unique signal that can sometimes be wrong.

7. **Insiders tend to buy early.** Investors have a few days or even weeks to buy shares. There's no need to rush in. However, most of the excess benefits from insider trading occur within three to six months. After 12 months, there is typically no additional benefit achievable from an insider trade.

8. **Smaller firms with insider buying tend to perform better than larger firms with insider buying.** Smaller companies tend to be off the radar, so insiders truly know best relative to Wall Street analysts who might not even recognize a company's existence.

9. **Investors can use call options to put less capital to work and achieve larger percentage gains with insider trades.** By using this money multiplier system, investors can turn the excess returns of insider buying into larger percentage gains to boost their wealth.

10. **Investors can sell put options to generate income to substantially boost their income.** Income-oriented investors

can take advantage of the statistical likelihood of insider buys to outperform the market to sell put options, a strategy that yields immediate income.

By following these key points and using them as guidelines, investors can maximize their benefit from following insider trades. They won't buy into every trade, and they'll reduce their chances of losing money from any single trade going awry.

Afterword: A Timeless, Yet Timely, Strategy

As a financial newsletter publisher, I'm constantly being told about the innumerable opportunities that exist for investors. I've heard all about the different ways to make big money in stocks, bonds, commodities, options, real estate — you name it.

Yet for every single financial newsletter that I've helped launch and create, I've rejected more than a dozen. That's because the strategy or premise is too narrow, too confusing, or too hard to make consistent, reliable returns. They simply don't work to help improve investment returns.

So you can imagine how surprised I was when I first started talking to Andrew Packer about insider trading. It's a strategy that's based on stocks, but it doesn't rely on a specific sector. It doesn't rely purely on valuation or technical analysis. It isn't beholden to the overall stock market rising or falling.

As you've read throughout this book, it's an over-simplification to say that buying alongside insiders beats the market. Andrew has revealed that if you look at specific groups of insiders and add in a few simple valuation and technical signs, you can eliminate the worst-performing insider trades to just focus on the top potential returns.

How do I trust that this strategy works so well? Because Andrew has been putting his own money to work to prove it. You've seen the evidence, too, since Andrew has used these examples throughout this book. Over the second half of 2013, Andrew slightly edged out the market's annual return in just a handful of trades. This included the purchase of Equal Energy (EQU), selling put options on Accenture (CAN) and Western Gas Partners (WES), call options on Pulte Homes (PHM), and a few more.

As a publisher, when I see an investment writer who "eats their own cooking," I know I'm looking at the real deal. Insider investing generates solid returns in a short amount of time. It can beat the market consistently. And with the use of options, it can help you meet your investment goals, whether it's to afford a vacation, a new car, or even make up for those down years that have held your retirement back.

I hope that you'll use this book as a jumping-off guide to improve your investment returns.

Of course, it's also a lot to soak in. There's a lot of knowledge out there regarding insider trading and it needs to be translated into useful trades. Even with this guide in your hands, I know full well as a financial publisher that most investors will want some hands-on help identifying the best insider trading opportunities.

That's why we created the *Insider Hotline* newsletter. Following the principles outlined in this book, Andrew will read through all the latest SEC filings on insider trading. That way, you don't have to. You'll be able to use his system to weed out the irrelevant trades, and focus only on those investments that have the best prospect of high-returns with low risk. He'll also identify options trades to turbo-charge your wealth. With its market-beating potential, taking advantage of this timeless, yet timely, strategy makes more sense than most investment strategies being touted right now.

Aaron DeHoog
Moneynews **publisher**